'Play is child's work...'

This book is the second in Susan's series of three practical guides to purposeful play for ages 3 to 5, written for both parents and practitioners.

Susan is a qualified teacher with a specialist pre-school qualification, a former nursery school proprietor and a former Childcare Education NVQ Assessor.

Thank you…

…first and foremost to my husband Ian for his support, encouragement and technical knowhow.

…to all the children featured in the book and their parents.

…to Francesca Dunning for her very professional work with the images and incorporating them within the text.

…to my daughter Liza for allowing me to turn her home temporarily and regularly into an activity centre.

…to my mother Meg who has always been interested in the progress of these three books. I lovingly dedicate this second book in the series to her and to the memories of my father Robin.

PLAY IS CHILD'S WORK

BOOK 2

Susan Conway

Bushbuck Books

Published in 2015 by Bushbuck Books

First Edition

ISBN: 978-0-9929744-1-1

Set in Palatino Linotype

Printed and bound in the United Kingdom by
Lightning Source UK Ltd., Milton Keynes.

Safety

This book contains recommendations, views and suggested activities in the context of early years education, together with certain safety precautions. Of course it would be impracticable to list every potential risk and precaution associated with every feature of the book, particularly having regard to the wide range of capabilities of children. Therefore in interpreting and using the recommendations and activities safely, it is very important that the reader is alert to safety implications and uses her common sense, her knowledge of her child's particular capabilities and her own experience.

If in doubt about using any of the recommendations and activities for her child, the reader should first seek professional childcare or medical advice as appropriate. It is implicit that all the activities must be supervised by a responsible adult.

'Play is the highest level of child development...'

F. Froebel (1782-1852)
Creator of Kindergarten

Contents

Introduction

My intention in writing this book, and the other two books in the series, is to show how you can engage your child to enable her all round development. Dip in and enjoy the book at random or use it as curriculum material for these two valuable early years.

The need to play is very strong for young children, and your child learns and makes sense of the world as she plays; hence the title 'Play is Child's Work'. She understands more about construction and shape, while developing cognitive ability and dexterity, when actually building, say, a palace from bricks. She learns best this way, involved first hand, and play suggestions in the book reflect this. I have expanded the traditional meaning of play, for the purpose of this book, to include relevant activities and the routine and events of daily life.

Curious about everything, the unusual and the humdrum, children delight in both planned and spontaneous experiences. Planning and provisioning play and activities is enjoyable, as well as taking opportunities as they arise. Having seen a use for the still perfect petals from a wilted rose, for example, I showed Ava how to tease them apart. In the photo she takes great pleasure throwing the petals in the air; watching and feeling them brush her as they float down. She used them again, creating a collage. Ideas in this book are there to be used directly, also to stimulate lateral thought so you take advantage of materials and situations unique to you.

I decided to use the words 'your child' throughout the book, instead of 'the child' because it is friendlier, more personal and applies equally well to parent and practitioner - the nanny's, childminder's charge or the child the nursery practitioner is currently interacting with. For descriptive purposes the gender of 'your child' alternates chapter by chapter.

The threes and fours can be a delightful age. As parent, carer, simply make the most of it, before she enters the more formal environs of school. As a practitioner your job is very important, and the more you see it as enjoyable and worthwhile the more effective the results for your child. Join in the play, games and activities; children are thrilled if you have the time and benefit from your input. When you stand back see both sole and group play leap in quality.

Children with special needs, I find, generally enjoy being with their peers who are usually empathetic, keen to look out for children who may need help. Joining in with peers, and soothing sensory experiences such as water play can increase confidence and wellbeing. Suggested activities and educational outcomes may be equally relevant to children with special needs. Assess the suitability of activities for your child with assistance, and extra equipment as appropriate, from your specialist advisors.

'Learning Outcomes' across curriculum areas are described at the end of chapters. Their relevancy depends on which activities you choose to do, how you adapt them etc. Too much emphasis on outcomes I feel makes play sterile and is unnecessary. Learning is a natural outcome of your child's inclination for new, repetition of old, well presented and spontaneous experiences - all taken at her own pace without pressure and fear of failure.

I hope you find what is offered truly inspirational, whether you choose to use these pages as curriculum material or for dipping in, perhaps via the index, and trying ideas at random.

1 Sounds, Rhymes and Songs

Sounds, rhymes and simple songs spell enjoyment for your pre-school child as she listens, moves and sings along.

Everyday Sounds

In The Home

Comment to your child how quiet it is inside, when other family members have left for work and school. 'Why was it so noisy?' 'Where did the sounds come from?' 'What or who made the sounds?' The home is full of sounds early in the morning: alarm clock ringing, taps running, feet on stairs, kettle boiling, cereal crackling, toast popping, shouts of 'hurry up', 'goodbye' and the front door slamming. Later on in the day she may hear the clump of bags thrown down, rustling of crisps, crunching of apples and from outside the whacking of footballs.

Outdoors

Listen with your child for sounds when out and about or from the setting's playground. Cats meowing, dogs barking, cows mooing, engines revving, lorries braking, machines whirring, sirens blaring. If she stays still and quiet, perhaps closing her eyes to avoid visual distraction, she might hear sounds she would otherwise miss: a distant boom, leaves fluttering (in the breeze), birds singing, bees buzzing, conkers plopping. At the weekend: church bells ringing, football/cricket fans cheering.

Audio Stories

AN AUDIO STORY COMES TO LIFE IF YOUR CHILD HEARS THE SOUND OF THE ENGINE REVVING, THE HORN TOOTING, THE HORSE NEIGHING.

Storybooks have illustrations to help bring the plot to life. Without pictures an audio story arouses her interest, she listens more closely when she hears the hens clucking rather than just being told this is happening by the narrator. Before buying an audio story, which should combine realistic sounds within a good plot, listen to extracts first, if you can. Recordings by authors such as Janet and Alan Alberg are worth looking out for.

Onomatopoeic Language

As a toddler your child loved to imitate sounds made by vehicles and animals. Now, she makes them part of imaginative play: 'vroom, vroom', as she pushes cars around, 'choo, choo', as her trains leave the station. Onomatopoeic words enrich descriptive language; she uses them naturally, encourage her further e.g. 'The rain is pittar-pattering against the window'. 'Does the rain sound a bit like that as it hits the glass?' 'What word can we make up that sounds like a baby crying?'

Sound Makers

Around The Home

In your home, you have the rudiments to enable your child to create a range of sounds. Stay in the vicinity to make suggestions and ask questions as your child experiments with turning objects, you have deemed safe, into sound makers. In the kitchen, apart from the proverbial pan and spoon loved by toddlers, wood, metal and plastic spoons can be tapped together, then against a metal tin, plastic tin, wooden rolling pin and so on.

TAPPING TWO SHELLS TOGETHER MAKES A SOFT CLACK.

Keep a few sound makers e.g. a couple of plastic baby spoons and wooden blocks for your child to tap together, baby bells, squeaker and a rattle to shake. Some unusual ones too, I keep a small hinged wooden box, children close it forcefully and gently producing loud and soft clacks. They find the top pulled repeatedly off my tin tube makes a series of satisfying pops.

Look in other rooms too; sliding her fingers or a stick slowly over grooved textured objects, e.g. a comb, a brush, rattan paper bin, she hears a series of repetitive sounds. When she strikes objects combining solid and hollow parts she hears different sounds emitted depending on where they are struck.

WHEN PLUCKED THE WIRES ON AN EGGSLICER PRODUCE A SATISFYING SOUND, NOT UNLIKE A HARP.

Making Sound Shakers

Make shakers using clean, empty plastic pots with lids. Place one type of dry uncooked food in each one; your child enjoys helping you choose from your cupboards. I made the six shakers overleaf with half a teaspoon of sugar, a few pumpkin seeds, a piece of macaroni, a dried pea, several grains of rice and one bay leaf. When you have fitted the last top on, decorate the shakers with bright coloured crepe paper.

Playing Sound Shakers

Let your child, in her own time, shake and listen to each shaker. She might like to close her eyes so she can concentrate on the sounds. Help her describe the sounds by asking which she likes best and which she likes least and if she can tell you why. For me, the sugar and rice shakers make pleasant soft, melodic sounds, while the pea and pasta shakers make harsh, loud sounds. Settings might like to make up pairs of shakers with matching contents, then ask the children to shake and listen carefully to all of them. 'Can they pick out the shakers with the same sounds?'

Leading Children in Singing

Your child is enchanted if you are prepared to sing to her. It is lucky, for most of us, that young children are less attuned to voice quality than whether we are enthusiastic about singing. If you show you are enjoying yourself your child is quick to respond and the more you sing, the better your singing becomes. Most nursery rhymes and songs have a natural rhythm making them easy to recite or sing. You could start by reading nursery rhymes with your child, many of which you may already know, gradually bringing inflexion and musicality to your voice. Listen to recordings of nursery rhymes and songs choosing those featuring clear children's voices or an adult singer with a natural non-operatic singing style. You soon remember the tunes and at settings continue singing along until you feel comfortable to lead a group without the aid of a recording.

The language of rhyme and song is fresh and fun for children, and books abound. 'This Little Puffin', by Elizabeth Matterson is a wonderful compilation of all the rhymes and songs practitioners could possibly want. You might like to write down or upload some favourites, and perhaps your child singing a rhyme or two; she is amused to hear herself on playback.

Traditional Rhymes and Songs

Traditional rhymes and songs have stood the test of time. They are popular still and connect your child with the past; having come down to us through the ages. The simple words, rhythms and repeated phrases in nursery rhymes and songs appeal directly to her. Singing is an ideal activity for settings where a number of children can take part together, sitting comfortably on chairs, arranged in a semicircle, facing you. In this arrangement children can see you singing and follow your actions. Children with roots abroad could bring their own traditional rhymes for everyone to try. In the taster selection of rhymes and songs below, children participate actively. At home sing rhymes together anywhere and if possible let her see your face clearly.

Action Rhymes

ONE, TWO, THREE, FOUR, FIVE

One, two, three, four, five,
Once I caught a fish alive,
Six, seven, eight, nine, ten,
Then I let it go again.
Why did you let it go?
Because it bit my finger so
Which finger did it bite?
This little finger on the right.

TWO LITTLE DICKY BIRDS

Two little dicky birds sitting on a wall,
One named Peter, one named Paul,
Fly away, Peter! Fly away, Paul!
Come back, Peter! Come back, Paul!

INCY WINCY SPIDER

Incy Wincy spider climbing up the spout,
Down came the rain and washed poor Incy out.
Out came the sunshine and dried up all the rain,
Incy Wincy spider climbed up the spout again.

LITTLE MOUSY BROWN

Your child holds her arm up for this rhyme too:
Up the tall white candlestick,
Crept little Mousy Brown,
Right to the top but she/he couldn't get down,
She/he called for her/his Grandma 'Grandma',
But her/his Grandma was in town,
So she/he curled herself/himself into a ball,
And rolled all the way down.

FIVE LITTLE PEAS

Five little peas in a pea-pod pressed,
One grew, two grew and so did all the rest.
They grew and grew and did not stop,
Until one day the pod went POP.
(Clap hands together on POP)

I'M A LITTLE TEAPOT

I'm a little teapot, short and stout,
Here's my handle, here's my spout.
When I see the teacups/steam come hear me shout,
'Tip me up and pour me out!'

FIVE CURRANT BUNS

This nursery song is ideal to play when your child has friends around and at group settings. Put out five 'baked playdough' buns and five shiny pennies. When each child hears their name, they get up, pick up a penny and purchase a bun from the baker until none are left (if there are six children one can be baker). Increase the number of buns and pennies by the number of children so everyone is included. Alternatively, involve the other children, by name, in another song.

Five currant buns in the baker's shop,
Round and fat with sugar on the top.
Along came Ben with a penny one day,
Bought a currant bun and took it away.
Reduce 4,3,2,1.

ONE FINGER ONE THUMB KEEP MOVING

Your child, as the words in the song imply, has to keep moving for this fast rhythmical song with lots of action.

One finger one thumb keep moving,
One finger one thumb keep moving,
One finger one thumb keep moving we'll all be merry and bright

One verse at a time add arm, leg, nod of the head, stand up, sit down.

With a Partner

For this you and your child sit on the floor facing each other, arms and legs outstretched in front, holding hands and with feet touching. Rock backwards and forwards in time to the song.

Row, row, row your boat,
Gently down the stream,
Merrily, merrily, merrily, merrily
Life is but a dream.

Row, row, row, your boat,
Gently out to sea,
Merrily, merrily, merrily, merrily,
We'll be home for tea.

Row, row, row your boat,
Gently on the tide,
Merrily, merrily, merrily, merrily,
To the other side.

Row, row, row your boat,
Gently back to shore,
Merrily, merrily, merrily, merrily,
Home for tea at four.

In a Circle

'Ring-a-ring o'roses' is a lovely simple old favourite; hold hands with your child and in a group have enough adults joining in to keep the circle moving along. Sing; as you skip or walk around in a circle, sink to the floor and jump up for the second verse.

Ring-a-ring o' roses,
A pocket full of posies,
A-tishoo! A-tishoo!
We all fall down.

The cows are in the meadow,
Lying fast asleep,
A-tishoo! A-tishoo!
We all jump up.

An alternative second verse:
Fishes in the water,
Fishes in the sea,
We all jump up,
With a one, two, three.

Personalising Songs

WHO IS WEARING A PRETTY GREEN TOP?

As in the rhyme 'Five Currant Buns', children love to hear a line of verse personal to them. At home and particularly at settings the clothes children wear are a good source of inspiration. With the children sitting around you, sing about the clothes they are wearing.
Who is wearing a pretty green top?
Ellie is wearing a pretty green top.
Who is wearing bright blue trousers?
George is wearing bright blue trousers.

Or, on another occasion:
What is Ted wearing today?
Ted is wearing a stripy blue top?
As you go round the group the children, copying your tune, start answering the questions themselves.

Children can introduce themselves to a new child starting the group, by singing their names e.g.
My name is Ebony; is Ebony, is Ebony.

THE RABBIT ON THE FARM GOES MUNCH, MUNCH, MUNCH

Adapt existing nursery songs to bring a visit alive; she enjoys adding her suggestions. After a trip to a farm and to the tune of 'The wheels on the bus go round and round':

The dog on the farm goes woof, woof, woof,
Woof, woof, woof; woof, woof, woof;
The dog on the farm goes woof, woof, woof,
All day long.

The rabbit on the farm goes munch, munch, munch, etc.

The cat on the farm goes miaow, miaow, miaow, etc.
The hen on the farm goes cluck, cluck, cluck, etc.

THIS IS THE WAY WE STRETCH UP TALL

Extend songs such as 'Here we go round the Mulberry Bush'. Skip around in a circle singing the first verse of 'Mulberry Bush' then let the group suggest actions for additional verses.

Here we go around the Mulberry Bush,
The Mulberry Bush, the Mulberry Bush,
Here we go round the Mulberry Bush
On a cold and frosty morning.

This is the way we stamp our feet,
Stamp our feet, stamp our feet,
This is the way we stamp our feet,
On a cold and frosty morning.

This is the way we clap our hands, put on gloves, jump about etc.

Your child sometimes sings, to herself, a line, or verse from rhymes she has learnt, proud of her success – sing a reply to her. Occasionally sing, instead of speaking, a sentence and make up funny songs and rhymes together.

Learning Outcomes

Music, Science, Technology, Creativity, Cognitive Processes

- Listens carefully to the sounds around her, indoors, outdoors, in stories and recordings
- Differentiates between the sounds around her
- Mimics interesting sounds and makes up her own
- Explores some everyday objects turning them into sound makers
- Discovers the sounds are different depending on the object struck, and whether she taps gently, or forcefully
- Finds an object containing solid, hollow, ridged parts – discovers it produces different sounds depending on where it is struck
- Makes simple shakers, listens to their sounds, finds matching sound pairs

Music, Cognitive Processes

- Sings along, moves with others to simple rhymes and songs
- Produces sounds as she claps and stamps in time to songs
- Absorbs the rhythmic quality of simple rhymes and songs
- Sings regularly reinforcing tune which she begins to follow
- Recites some verses or lines from memory often to herself
- Makes up the odd line or two of song/rhyme

Physical Skills

- Moves body, particularly arms, hands and feet during action rhymes
- Moves with partner and in a circle, freely, stopping and starting as requested
- Sings – inhaling and exhaling air, strengthening muscles, increasing lung capacity

The World Around, Personal Qualities

- Listens attentively to sounds, rhymes and nursery songs
- Connects to the past via traditional rhymes and to the present with new songs
- Concentrates on joining in with songs and action rhymes broadening attention span
- Responds to the pleasure and emotion of songs and rhymes
- Socialises with others at settings during singing sessions
- Begins (particularly as a reluctant or shy speaker) to join in, gradually to sing, increasing confidence
- Experiences a sense of wellbeing as sings (with you or with a group)

Language and Literacy

- Appreciates the rhythm, humour and nonsense of nursery rhymes and songs
- Enriches her language through repetition of quirky rhymes and songs
- Enjoys language, extends vocabulary with rhymes and songs
- Imitates sounds of things around her - living, natural, and mechanical

Mathematics

- Holds up the appropriate number of fingers as she recites or sings numbers, in rhymes and songs
- Counts backwards, using her fingers, where the number is reduced with each verse ('5 currant buns' '5 little monkeys')
- Recites or sings rhymes and songs - some words/phrases normally, some with emphasis, others quickly or slowly
- Repeats the pattern/rhythm in subsequent verses which helps with counting and appreciating number patterns
- Claps, stamps in time to the rhythm in songs and rhymes
- Moves clockwise in circle dancing (Time and Shape)

2

Music, Instruments and Movement

Playing instruments, playing them to accompany songs, joining in music making and moving her body imaginatively to music are all simple enjoyments for your child.

Musical Instruments

Add some other instruments to your collection of sound makers, e.g. sandblocks, smooth and ridged rhythm sticks, tambourine, drum, triangle, cymbals, handbells, castanets, chime bar. A drum or tambourine is a popular purchase at home; parchment or skin is used, for better sound quality, on the more expensive ones. Just a few good instruments suffice at home, whereas settings could build their collection, including unusual examples, and guarantee musical quality by purchasing through an educational supplier.

Exploring Musical Instruments

Your child makes many discoveries for himself by playing freely with the instruments. Make suggestions, occasionally, which encourage him to use the instruments in ways that might not occur to him. Ask him to hit an instrument a couple of times then immediately hit another and another. He can compare the different sounds produced. Striking one instrument in different places can also produce a range of sounds.

Suggest he selects an instrument and varies the way he normally plays it. For example, he shakes and hits the tambourine but has he tried rotating it slowly, beating it with his palm and tapping it with his fingers? Has he tried sliding the beater along the chime bar producing a series of notes from high to low, low to high? Has he discovered how to hold the triangle properly? If he holds the metal part of the triangle when he strikes it with the steel rod he hears a very tinny sound. If he holds the triangle by the attached string, when he strikes with the rod, he hears a pleasant tingly sound, altogether different. Castanets are difficult for him to manipulate; he still has fun trying and satisfaction when he produces the 'clack clack' sounds.

Sounds Ending, Stopping Sounds

Strike a chime bar or triangle and ask your child to tell you when the sound has completely faded away. After listening to the end, he is aware how long it takes for the note to completely fade. Strike the triangle and ask your child to stop the sound by putting his finger on the triangle. This time, by intervening, he stops the note immediately.

Loud and Soft Sounds

Often, children's initial inclination is to play instruments vigorously producing loud sounds. Ask him if he can produce soft sounds on drum, tambourine or triangle, to do so he finds he has to exert self-control and just apply gentle pressure. He can make even softer sounds by using his fingertips instead of the beater. It may intrigue him to discover that when home-made shakers containing grains of sugar and rice are shaken forcefully they still emit soft quiet sounds, unlike commercial shakers (maracas).

Let your child select a drum, triangle or tambourine to play along to this rhyme, making both loud and soft sounds. Recite the verse as he plays along, beating, striking or shaking the instrument vigorously for thunder and gently (tapping or rocking the instrument) for pitter-pattering raindrops.

I hear thunder, I hear thunder,
Hark don't you, Hark don't you?
Pitter-patter raindrops, Pitter-patter raindrops,
I'm wet through, So are you!

Sing this gentle song very softly for your child to play along to:
Lavender's blue, dilly-dilly,
Rosemary's green,
When I am King, dilly-dilly,
You shall be Queen.

Slow and Fast Sounds

Recite the rhyme, 'My Grandfather Clock' (or 'My Big Clock') for your child. The 'Tick Tock' of the Grandfather clock is slow and the 'Tick Tock' of the Grandmother clock (or small clock) is quick, twice as fast as the Grandfather clock.

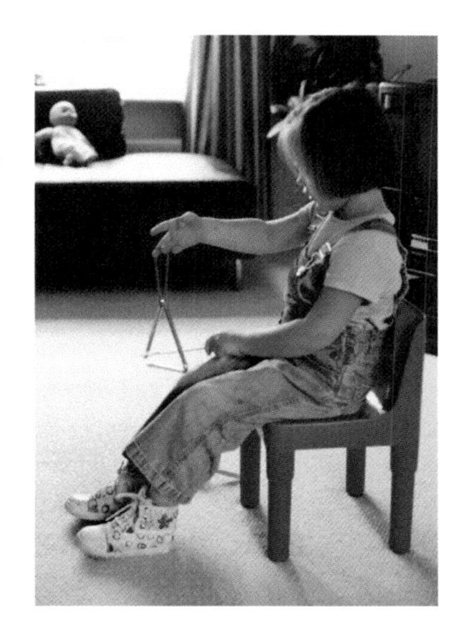

My Grandfather clock goes tick tock, tick tock,
My Grandmother clock goes tick-tock tick-tock, tick-tock tick-tock

Your child likes to copy and join in with you. As you recite the lines clap out the slow and quick 'Tick Tocks' together. Doing this enables him to keep in time and to experience how slow and fast sounds can create an interesting rhythm. Later he could play an instrument in time to the 'Tick Tocks'; the words help him to keep going along at the right speed.

Playing Along To Verse

IF YOU'RE HAPPY AND YOU KNOW IT

In this song your child uses hands and feet as instruments, as he claps and stamps. After hearing you sing, clapping and stamping at the appropriate times, he is eager to join in. He begins to understand that he has to listen attentively to the words for his cue to start clapping or stamping.

If you're happy and you know it, clap your hands, (Clap, clap)
If you're happy and you know it, clap your hands, (Clap, clap)
If you're happy and you know it
And you really want to show it,
If you're happy and you know it,
clap your hands! (Clap, clap)

If you're happy and you know it,
stamp your feet etc.

HICKORY DICKORY DOCK

As you recite the rhyme your child plays an instrument; raising it high in the air as the mouse runs up the clock and bringing it back again as the mouse runs down. When he feels confident he might join you in reciting the rhyme as well as playing the instrument.

Hickory Dickory Dock,
The mouse ran up the clock;
The clock struck One,
The mouse ran down,
Hickory Dickory Dock.

THE GRAND OLD DUKE OF YORK

Following the words of the song, your child raises and lowers the instrument twice, finishing off at waist height. Play an instrument yourself to begin with so he can follow your actions in time with the words.

The Grand old Duke of York, (waist height)
He had ten thousand men,
He marched them up, to the top of the hill, (raised above head)
And he marched them down again, (lowered to floor)
And when they were up they were up, (raised above head)
And when they were down they were down, (lowered to floor)
And when they were only half way up,
They were neither up nor down. (waist height)

Accompanying Personalised Songs

Children love to hear their own names in a song and these verses are sure to give a lot of pleasure. At settings a group of up to six children is ideal with each child picking a different instrument. Sing the verses, to any tune, and include each child's name as it comes round to their verse. If necessary, alter the verses according to the instruments you have available. Each child listens carefully for their name and has the instrument ready. At home your child picks up a fresh instrument for each verse. The instrument is played when you are singing the action lines - help children understand at what point to start and finish playing with this practice verse.

We can play the instruments,
This is the way we do it, (start clapping with first clap)
Clap, clap, clap,
Clap, clap, clap.

Ruby can play the big bass drum,
This is the way she does it,
Boom, boom, boom,
(hit drum with first 'Boom')
Boom, boom, boom.

Jack can play the castanets,
This is the way he does it,
Click, click, click,
Click, click, click.

Chloe can play the triangle,
This is the way she does it,
Ting, ting, ting,
Ting, ting, ting.

George can play the tambourine,
This is the way he does it,
Rattle, rattle, rattle,
Rattle, rattle, rattle.

Tilly can play the shaker,
This is the way she does it,
Shake, shake, shake,
Shake, shake, shake.

Sam can play the tinkly bells,
This is the way he does it,
Ring, ring, ring,
Ring, ring, ring.

Mia can play the wood/en blocks,
This is the way she does it,
Clack, clack, clack,
Clack, clack, clack.

Len can play the chime bar,
This is the way he does it,
Tap, tap, tap,
Tap, tap, tap.

Sound Patterns

Exploring simple musical instruments, singing rhymes and listening to music gives your child a feeling for rhythm; he is interested in and may spontaneously start creating sound patterns. Remind him of the simple 'Tick Tock' patterns of the fast and slow clocks then tap the patterns out on instruments. Tap out another simple sound pattern e.g. 'slow slow quick quick slow' for him to tap back to you. He finds it funny if you repeat the sound message back again.

Music and Movement

He hears music as background when the radio is on, tuned to a music channel, when your recordings are playing and as he watches children's TV. The latter's introductory tune might be the signal for him to sit and start watching. Listening to the soundtrack of a film seen and enjoyed, without visual distraction, he is even more aware of the melodies. Let him shake rattle and roll his sound makers along to the music he hears.

Children generally love to dance freely to music. Your child moves and shakes his body spontaneously especially if you join in wholeheartedly with him. He understands it is natural to move in response to music and is soon confident to dance on his own. Dancing to up-beat music is always popular, though playing music of many moods and tempos (see the list below) results in a greater range and more expressive movement.

Selecting the Music for Movement

Choose from a range of music genres: popular, classical, traditional jazz, ceremonial/triumphal, brass band pieces, courtly/medieval and country/folk. Choose a mix of tempo, pitch and strength in your selection - of classical music in particular:

- Pieces beginning quietly, gradually getting louder, finally reaching a crescendo
- Pieces beginning slowly, gradually becoming livelier, then slower again
- Quiet, soft pieces,
- Pieces with lots of bass notes;
- Quick pieces with high notes
- Pieces with notes ascending the scale and descending the scale
- Pieces where notes jump all over the scale
- Slow heavy pieces
- Up tempo pieces

Listening to the Music Together

At settings, occasionally listen with the children to the selected pieces of music; 'What does the music make you think of or remind you of?' 'How does it make you feel?' 'What does it make you want to do? Children may say that quiet soft music makes them feel floppy - discovering one of the benefits of music – that it can be relaxing as well as stimulating. Quick fast light music may set them jigging, wishing to get up and dance. A slow heavy piece may seem sad to them; I know a child who describes this music as grumpy and has a grumpy dance to accompany such pieces. Quick music with high notes may make them feel happy.

Expressive Imaginative Movement

A FAIRY DANCE DVD IS THE INSPIRATION FOR THE DANCING HERE.

Create some space at home for movement. Settings may have a room or hall available and a hand held computer is useful, the menu taking you quickly to the pieces you need. Help children to interpret the pieces with a few ideas to start off or join in yourself - children enjoy that. The following movements arise naturally from the music selections suggested above, contrasting tempos and moods enable children to continue on their own - altering their movements as the music leads them.

- Curl up small as the music quietly begins, stretching tall as it strengthens and flutter down (leaf, petal, butterfly) as the music softens
- Be the wind blowing, a dragon breathing fire, vehicles bustling around and the sun rising
- Move expressing the seasons, cycle of nature, growth, seed to flower, cocoon to butterfly
- Be bustling pedestrians, the traffic, or a train, in a city waking up becoming busy and still again at day end
- Be jungle animals, toys, astronauts, pirates, fairies and goblins

- Zig-zag across the room/space to staccato pieces (disconnected notes)
- Scamper around to quick music in a high register

- Make tippy-toe footsteps to soft pieces, not to wake anyone
- Make heavy ponderous large footsteps to music with lots of bass notes
- Walk, jump, run, swing, slide, skip, gallop according to tempo
- Walk regally, tall and straight to ceremonial music
- March, 'left right, left right, about turn' to military brass band pieces

Props

A few props can extend the possibilities for imaginative movement. With small bells strung onto elastic wrist or ankle bands your child, just like the nursery rhyme, 'has music wherever he goes'. With a mat he flies away on a magic carpet and with wings he is a goblin, fairy or even a fairy princess.

DARCY MOVES AND THE SCARF FOLLOWS, CREATING LINEAR SHAPES.

A light chiffon or silky translucent scarf, a crepe-paper or ribbon streamer held in the hand encourages your child to move arms and hands (and body) expressively, especially dancing to soft mood music. Collect props for safety reasons as soon as he has finished dancing.

Singing and Playing Instruments to Accompany Movement

I know someone who hums the lively tune 'Lord of the Dance' to encourage expressive movement. Others strum a guitar, or other instrument to accompany children's movement. Most of us need a little help and these verses have a natural rhythm making it easy to bring musicality to the voice. The repetition helps; it also affords time for your child to make the movements before the next verse.

I WENT TO SCHOOL ONE MORNING

I went to school one morning and I walked like this, walked like this, walked like this,
I went to school one morning and I walked like this,
All on my way to school.

Ask your child who or what he might meet on the way:

I met a squirrel jumping and he jumped like this,
Jumped like this, jumped like this,
I met a squirrel jumping and he jumped like this,
All on my way to school.

I met a pony galloping and she galloped like this,
Galloped like this, galloped like this,
I met a pony galloping and she galloped like this,
All on my way to school.

Continue until he has had enough and finish with:
I heard the school bell ringing and I ran like this,
Ran like this, ran like this,
I heard the school bell ringing and I ran like this,
All on my way to school.

CHILDREN AT SETTINGS NEED SPACE FOR MOVEMENT HERE 'SIMON SAYS' WORKS IN A CONFINED AREA FOR A SHORT PERIOD.

At settings children can play instruments for others to move to; at home too when your child has friends around. Beat a drum: young children find it fun to line up, march, turn right/left, stop, about turn, following orders or the leader as the drums roll. A drum or boots clumped together loudly and slowly sound beats for giant footsteps. Bells, triangle or gently shaken tambourine make a tinkle sound to accompany tiptoe steps. Sticks tapped together make a clip clop sound to accompany children trotting around as horses.

Learning Outcomes

Music, Science, Technology

- Explores freely a range of simple musical instruments
- Strikes, beats, taps, slides, shakes and clicks the instruments
- Listens closely and compares the sounds they make
- Strikes an instrument producing different sounds depending on where it is hit

- Hears some notes stop quickly and others gradually fade away
- Produces loud, soft, fast and slow notes
- Hears a range of notes between high and low as he strikes and slides the beater over the chime bar
- Stops and starts playing the instruments on cue
- Plays instruments to accompany verse and movement
- Taps out simple rhythms on the musical instruments

Music, Physical Skills, Creativity

- Dances spontaneously and freely to music and songs
- Moves imaginatively and expressively to music
- Describes different pieces of music as sad, happy, relaxing
- Listens and interprets the music's mood and tempo in dance
- Mimes actions of people, animals, objects, the cycle of nature
- Uses props to aid and extend expressive movement
- Demonstrates spatial awareness during movement to music
- Manipulates instruments developing fine co-ordination skills

Personal Qualities

- Listens attentively stopping and starting playing instruments on cue
- Exerts self-control as follows your instructions for music making
- Responds to the pleasure and emotion of listening and moving to music
- Joins in music making and movement with others
- Feels important when his name is sung increasing his confidence
- Finds music relaxing as well as stimulating

Language and The World Around

- Expresses in words what contrasting pieces of music remind him of, how they make him feel and how they make him want to move

- Brings his ideas and expresses your ideas in movement e.g. walking regally, being a jungle animal

Number

- Taps out simple rhythms on musical instruments
- Produces a rhythm pattern e.g. two slow beats on his drum followed by three quick taps and repeated - helps with counting and appreciating number patterns
- Claps and stamps using his hands and feet as instruments in time to the music- helps with counting and appreciating number patterns

Special Needs

All learning outcomes in chapters 1, 2, 3, 4 may apply; the learning outcomes below may be particularly appropriate.

- Joins in singing, movement and music making with others
- Sings rhymes inhaling exhaling air, clapping in time, moving arms, hands, feet and whole body in partner/circle rhymes
- Absorbs rhythm, humour and nonsense of rhymes and songs
- Counts backwards using her fingers as sings number rhymes
- Responds to the pleasure and emotion of listening to music
- Expresses (in words) what contrasting pieces of music remind him of, how they make him feel (sad, happy, relaxed)
- Moves and dances spontaneously and freely to music
- Explores a range of simple musical instruments
- Feels important when his name is sung (personalised verse)
- Enjoys the creativity and freedom, and feels a sense of wellbeing, through engagement in art activities.
- Explores painting, printing, collage and collage techniques using a range of tools and materials, in 2 and 3 dimensions.
- Produces texture, relief, tonal effects, shapes, lines, patterns
- Discovers art can be leisurely and relaxing, joins adults and other children at the art table, chatters extending language and social skills as the artwork/picture progresses.

3

Painting and Collage

Your child enjoys the creative freedom associated with painting. She enjoys exploring, selecting and fixing together different materials to create collage. She is fascinated by the physical properties of paint and glue. The glue dripping from her paste-stick and the paint-trail left after sweeping her paint-laden brush across paper. She is taken up, particularly early on, with the processes of the activity rather than the end result. Although absorbed in a painting she might not welcome interruptions revel in sharing some of the artistic experiences with your child.

AVA DECORATES A CROWN WITH COLLAGE PIECES SHE HAS CUT OUT.

Preparation

Protective Clothing

Long sleeved knee length painting overalls in washable nylon, with elasticated neck and cuffs are practical. Alternatively a home made painting smock can be made from an old adult shirt. Cut the collar off and trim sleeves to your child's arm length. Sew a hem 1cm to 2cm wide at neck and cuffs leaving openings to thread through a safety pin with elastic tape attached. Release the safety pin, sew the elastic tape ends together, finish the hems and put the smock on your child back to front then button up. If your child does not like getting messy or putting an overall on let her paint in her oldest clothes.

Where to Paint and Collage?

Your child has freedom of movement standing at an easel to paint; make sure, if purchasing one, it has a shelf wide enough to hold paint pots. Painting on paper fixed to a (messy) wall or on the floor, with newspaper underneath, also meets her space requirements. Attach a large sheet of paper, to the easel or wall, with masking tape, which is easily removed. Make sure you have a large plastic cover or plenty of newspaper not only underfoot but adjacent to where she is working - paint has a habit of splashing further than you think. For safety, replenish the newspaper if it gets wet and dry the plastic cover. For collage, and the art activities in the next chapter a space on the floor or on a child size table is ideal, cover with newspaper first. Children enjoy clearing away, mopping up and so on; expect your child to help.

Arranging Displays

WRITE LABELS FOR WALL DISPLAYS; SEE MORE IN CHAPTER 4 ART ACTIVITIES. OCCASIONALLY DRAW YOUR CHILD'S ATTENTION TO THE DISPLAYS CHATTING ABOUT THEM AND READING THE PRINT.

Display your child's pictures in a scrapbook, from a string line using pegs, on a kitchen cupboard, wallboard and so on. She can write her name, a caption too, if appropriate, on each picture; or you could write the words for her to copy. Settings can purchase large rolls of frieze paper and corrugated paper in bright colours useful for group displays. For safety blutac and double sided tape are preferable to pins for attaching pictures to displays.

Painting Preparation

Paper

During painting your child enjoys making large strokes, her chunky brush thick with colour. Small sheets of paper can be restrictive, try to find big sheets to accommodate her brushstrokes, e.g. inexpensive art pads, the back of wallpaper roll-ends, lining paper and packing paper. Settings can purchase newsprint paper cheaply from an educational supplier; it can be ordered flat in a choice of sizes or by the roll - you rip off what you need. Widen her experience by occasionally providing coloured paper. Gold, silver, bronze metallic paints and florescent paints, which come in a wide range of colours, can be very effective when painted on vivid papers.

Powder Water Paint, Brushes and Pots

Choose water-soluble non-toxic children's paint, available as powder or ready mixed. Avoid block paint, although less messy it is less satisfying for your child to use. The ready mixed paint is convenient, although powder is better value if you intend to have paint out frequently. Look for short chunky paintbrushes, for an easy grip and more control, with thick bristles for the large strokes she enjoys making. Paint pots invariably get knocked over so buy the non-spill variety, with stoppers to prevent any remaining paint, you wish to save, from drying out.

PAINTING OUTSIDE IN THE FRESH AIR IS FUN. DARCY IS USING CLEAN RECYCLED PACKING PAPER.

Mixing Powder Paint

The water mixes more effectively with the powder paint if it is added gradually. Put two heaped tablespoonfuls of powder into a paint pot, add a couple of tablespoons of warm water and stir until thoroughly mixed in. Add more water until a fairly thick consistency is achieved. As you stir, and your child watches the water absorbing the powder, talk to her about what is happening. Another time, with your help, she could try mixing the paint herself.

Decrease or increase quantities to fit your requirements, bearing in mind that although the pots of paint start off bright and colourful, they may be muddy coloured by session end. If you want to reuse any paint left over insert the rubber stoppers, preventing the remaining paint from drying out, and stir thoroughly before using next time. Gradually introduce other colours in future painting sessions. For a different effect try children's gold, silver, bronze metallic paints and florescent paints in a wide range of colours.

Secondary Colours

THE PRIMARY COLOURS RED AND YELLOW MAKE THE SECONDARY COLOUR ORANGE; YELLOW AND BLUE MAKE GREEN AND RED AND BLUE MAKE PURPLE.

At some point, broaden her range of colours by introducing secondary colours. You can buy them, but it is worthwhile for your child to mix the paint herself to produce the new colours. The primary colours combine in unequal measures to produce the secondary colours, you need to experiment. I get through a large quantity of yellow powder because green paint takes a lot of yellow powder and just a touch of blue.

Painting

Your child expresses herself freely through the medium of paint recording pictorially what she wants, what she knows and what she has seen. At first, brush strokes take the form of lines, squiggles and spots, then later rough circles and other shapes. Later still lines are painted from these shapes to represent arms and legs, with detail such as facial features, hair, hands and feet included over time.

Early Paintings

Put out red, yellow and blue paint in non-spill paint pots with three chunky paintbrushes. Show her how to replace the brushes in the pots; the brush with red paint goes back in the red paint pot and so on. You may find; even if she manages to put the brushes back correctly, the colours soon take on a muddy appearance, as do her pictures. Vibrant colours suddenly become a muddy mess as she paints over the top of previous brushstrokes swirling them altogether. In the early stages of painting the process is far more important to her than the end result.

Later Paintings

Much later, although the experience itself remains important her pleasure extends to the artistic effect produced. She becomes accustomed to applying paint to paper and shows more interest in the final result; pictures start to retain their original colours. At this stage, if she is wondering what to paint, you could suggest subjects she knows well: Herself (she can look in a mirror), you, other family members, her home, the sun, sky, trees, buildings, vehicles and pets. She may like to paint pictures of things she has read about with you that interest her; e.g. robots and machines.

When she brings paintings to you to admire, instead of simply saying, 'That's nice', which can seem a bit trite after a while, pick out an aspect or aspects of the picture to comment on. This encourages her more effectively; e.g. 'I like the ripples in your sea picture – very realistic'. If you are not sure of the subject, she may not, anyway, be attempting to represent anything in particular make your comments less specific e.g. 'The bright red shapes really stand out'.

3D Painting

PAINT CAN BRING CONSTRUCTIONS ALIVE; THE CROCODILE, IN THE PHOTO, IS ONLY RECOGNISABLE AS SUCH, WHEN PAINT IS APPLIED.

The crocodile is made from egg boxes, shoeboxes and cardboard tubes glued together, given bulk with papier mache and transformed with green paint. 3 dimensional painting is a new experience for your child; she has to work her way around the piece, paint pot in hand, checking she has covered every nook and cranny.

Collage Materials

A Range of Papers

Crepe, tissue, corrugated, textured and decorative papers available in various colours, sizes, shapes and weights are ideal for collage activities, together with smaller pieces such as stars and other pre-cut shapes. These materials, together with sugar paper and card which provide a base for attaching materials can be found in art shops and other shops on the 'High Street'. Rolls of sugar paper and card, to cut as required, and for individual use, multicoloured packs of sugar paper and card can be purchased from educational suppliers.

Natural Materials

Some natural materials e.g. conkers, acorns, fruit seeds, leaves, twigs, are perishable with a short life; they are fun to collect and glue down to create a seasonal picture. When outdoors, looking for natural materials encourage her to look closely at veins in a leaf, texture on tree bark and so on.

Recycled materials

Look critically at what you may consider to be rubbish before throwing away, it could be ideal for collage, e.g. raffia and ribbon tying a bouquet together. Recycling suitable materials adds variety to the basic stock enriching the creative experience. Seek out a wide range of materials; settings could ask for unwanted samples, end of lines, remnants, at wallpaper and fabric shops. They could also bump up their stocks by letting parents know they need clean unused fabric, wool remnants, clean and dry recycled items, such as cellophane bouquet wrapping and so on.

Dry uncooked out of date foodstuffs can be used successfully for

collage activities: rice, pasta shapes, pulses, nuts, sunflower, pumpkin and poppy seeds and so on. One parent, at my setting, proudly displayed her child's collage on the wall at home, only to find it, to her amusement and disbelief, lying decimated on the floor the next morning - the oats and raisons had proved irresistible to the family dog. The moral of the story; you can't explain 'eat by date' to pets. Explain to your child that the items are not edible and check that she is gluing away not munching away.

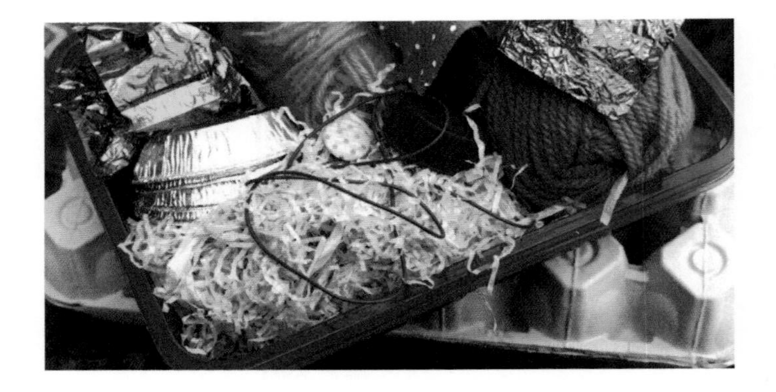

Collect:

- Miscellaneous odds and ends you have finished with: buttons, ribbon, sweet wrappers, string, wool, embroidery silks, beads and so on
- Paper oddments: wrapping, silver, tissue, crepe, textured, decorative, shredded, cellophane and wallpaper
- Fabric bits: patterned, plain, coloured, natural, fleece, leather, faux fur, plastic, chiffon, velvet, silk
- Fabric: translucent, opaque, water repellent and stretchy

For other sources of collage materials, raid items collected for printing activities (see chapter 4 Art Projects for list) and the larger items saved for junk construction. For example, large cardboard boxes, sheets of cardboard, egg boxes, clean plastic food trays, foil inner tubes, chocolate box dividers, circular cheese boxes, card and cardboard packaging.

Organising Collage Materials

It is fun for your child to empty out a full container of paraphernalia, to rummage through and chat about the items. Organising the materials at some point, though, is usually necessary, for settings at least. Divide by category, e.g. fabric. When the fabric box starts bulging, rather than changing to a larger box which would contain too much fabric to choose from and be too heavy to carry comfortably, I subdivide by fabric colour. If lucky enough to have to subdivide again I separate according to colour and pattern; e.g. green check, green stripe, green floral etc. I don't throw resources away, they are too precious, and at settings stock can quickly become depleted.

Sorting Small Materials

Small collage materials such as bottle tops and buttons are applied whole, just as they are. They can be sorted by attribute into receptacles such as clean ice cream or margarine tubs; involve your child in this activity. Start her off by putting an example item, for her to follow, in each tub. When she is finished the tubs can be slotted on top of each other and stored away. Another sorting opportunity arises when, for example, a button tub is full; she can subdivide the buttons into a number of smaller tubs according to colour, pattern or even texture – leather, silk and cotton.

Exploring Collage Materials

Let her rifle through the collage materials, during sorting and sticking sessions. Discuss materials using descriptive vocabulary; she soon follows your lead. Her senses are heightened - as she smoothes out sweet wrappers, breathes aromas of lavender, feels the scratchiness of hessian, the ridges and indentations of embossed paper.

Making Discoveries

Let her compare a selection of fabric remnants making discoveries about their properties. Discuss what is happening, as you help her attempt to stretch them, as she dips them in water and holds them up to the light. She discovers some fabrics stretch, others do not; some repel water others absorb water; some fabrics are transparent, others opaque.

Applying Collage Materials

PVA glue

PVA glue is ideal for collage activities; it is capable of sticking the collage items mentioned below, and in the next chapter, onto card, paper and even some plastic surfaces. It is white and viscous when applied, clear and glossy when dry. Avoid the glue running, leaving a shiny trail which could spoil the picture by placing completed collages flat on a surface until completely dry. PVA glue is widely available; to avoid running out of it buy medium or large size tubs. Settings can purchase extra-large sizes from educational suppliers. A glue stick is sometimes attached to the pot lid, but plastic glue-sticks are inexpensive, less messy and easier to use. A child's pair of scissors is essential for cutting collage; do supervise her closely. See Book 3 Chapter 2 Fine Physical Skills for more cutting activities.

Being Creative with Collage Materials

During her early collage attempts your child is fascinated by the glue, she watches the viscous white liquid flow from glue-stick to puddles on paper - expect sparsely collaged pictures. Allow for experimentation with a limited selection of collage materials to begin with, gradually introducing a wider range. As she continues to handle glue and materials she becomes more accustomed and appreciative of their physical properties and creative potential.

GLUING BITS OF SPARKLY SILVER CARD ONTO A PLAIN CROWN. AND BELOW, STICKING BEADS AND OTHER COLLAGE BITS TO MAKE A CARD.

Over time she might start to think about how she would like to arrange the materials; what type of collage she would like to produce; where she could find extra materials; when she should cut, with your help, the larger materials. Perhaps she decides on a pattern, representational picture or to decorate something plain choosing the materials carefully, arranging the pieces paying attention to how they appear before gluing in position.

Learning Outcomes

Chapter 3 Painting and Collage

Personal, Artistic, Creative, Sensory

- Expresses herself through the medium of paint and collage
- Enjoys the creativity and freedom associated with painting and the application of collage
- Taken up with the processes of the artistic activity concerned, much later, applies materials to produce a pleasing effect
- Paints lines, swirls, curves, spots, shapes and representations of people, animals, buildings, objects etc. from experience
- Transforms 3D junk constructions with paint
- Handles and closely observes a wide spectrum of materials
- Selects, arranges and fixes materials to create collage pictures
- Sees how materials can be transformed in creative endeavour
- Explores materials of varying textures, hues and patterns

Personal Qualities

- Discovers art can be leisurely, relaxing and satisfying
- Feels a sense of wellbeing through engagement in art
- Joins adults and other children at the art table enhancing social skills as she converses and progresses her picture
- Self-reliant - makes decisions on subject matter and materials
- Produces pictures she likes and feels proud about, bringing an increase in confidence
- Concentrates when immersed in paint and collage play
- Revels in the chance to get messy (some children not so keen)
- Helps with clearing away chores, as appropriate
- Shows patience as she waits for artwork to dry

Language, Fine Physical Skills

- Communicates with other children and adults at the art table

- Continues the process of colour recognition and naming
- Uses descriptive vocabulary when describing materials
- Observes detail as she paints, prints; selects and applies collage (experience for letter shape and word recognition)
- Recognises her name and captions on displayed pictures
- Develops control over fine movements as she handles paintbrushes, glue sticks, printing tools, scissors, collage bits
- Cut, tears or breaks materials into manageable proportions

Cognitive Processes, Mathematics

- Stretches her brain as she decides what to paint, materials and tools to use, how to use them and where to use them
- Develops an open-ended lateral approach as she sifts materials, assessing possibilities
- Sorts collage materials according to attributes
- Groups and arranges materials for a picture
- Creates pattern and repeated pattern
- Applies paint and collage in rough geometric shapes and in a more accurate form with pre-cut examples
- Paints and creates collage in two and three dimensions
- Explores proportion as she paints people and things
- Experiences the relationship between shape and space as she paints and applies collage
- Uses mathematical language e.g. light, heavy, thin, thick as she handles materials

Science, The World Around

She discovers that:

- Paint powders become liquid when combined with water
- Paint powder colours water
- Paint is thick or thin according to quantity of powder mixed into the water
- Mixing two primary colours produces a new (secondary) colour

- Paints have different finishes e.g. metallic, glossy, matt, luminous
- Glue is a white viscous liquid when freshly coating her paste brush and transparent and hard when dry
- Fabrics and papers can be stretchable, water repellent, absorbent, translucent
- Paint, papers, fabrics, natural (e.g. lavender) and recycled materials provide a rich sensory experience
- Veins in a leaf, textures on tree bark, brick pattern in buildings (aware of detail features in her surroundings)

Chapter 4 Art Activities

Most of the learning outcomes from chapter three apply here with the following additional outcomes.

Artistic/Creative, Aesthetic, Sensory

- Explores printing, painting and collage techniques using a range of tools and materials
- Produces texture, relief and tonal effects, circles and other shapes, line, pattern and decorative features
- Prints with natural and man-made tools on various materials
- Notices imprints are bright initially gradually fading with each successive imprint
- Discovers paint appearance varies according to tools used, thickness or thinness of mixture, application of heavy or light pressure, amount of paint remaining on the tool
- Interested in the seemingly magical results with oil paint
- Arranges and applies materials to produce a pleasing effect
- Chooses elements from different mediums to create pictures

Language, Literacy and Mathematics

- Discusses the possibilities materials offer and what he hopes to achieve with them
- Extends language during convivial chatter with others

- Observes detail in paint effects and as he selects and applies collage - experience for letter shape and word recognition
- Prints with geometric shaped printing tools e.g. cotton reel and applies pre-cut geometric paper shapes during collage
- Aware gradually of pattern in his pictures, created initially in a haphazard way and later in a more planned way – experience for number (multiplication)
- Explores paint and collage in two and three dimensions
- Finds or much later decides on spacing between and around collage and printing applications – spatial awareness

Science (Sensory Experiences)

- Feels slightly raised areas caused by printing and collage
- Observes particles of oil paint suspended in water
- Concludes oil paint does not dissolve unlike powder paint
- Paints one side of a sheet of paper presses it down on other half producing a mirror image (a symmetrical painting)
- Removes paint from tools by immersing in warm water

Discovers:

- Foam is a highly absorbent material
- Air blown through paint moves it in different directions
- Air blown through paint mixed with washing up liquid produces bubbles
- Textural effects are achieved by the gaps and holes in printing tools e.g. comb, sponge
- Deeper colour tones and new colours are visible where oil paints intermingle
- Overlapping pieces of translucent coloured paper or fabric create a new colour or darker shade

4

Art Activities

During paint and collage activities, your child uses a range of tools techniques and materials sometimes combining them in mixed media projects. At home, when you organise art activities and have a spare moment, sit with him to chat about what he is doing. At settings children benefit from an adult to talk to, as they progress through the activity. Paint and collage activities should be leisurely and relaxed, your child happy to seek your opinion; discussing the possibilities materials offer and what he hopes to achieve with them.

Printing with Tools

Preparation

For your child, printing involves using a tool and paint to make an imprint on a surface. Some of the best tools to experiment with are undamaged household bits and pieces; e.g. plastic bottle tops, cotton reels, foam oddments, toy threading beads and worn plastic bricks. Settings can supplement their collection with purchased printing tools. Fruit and vegetables can be carved to the shape you want before printing, particularly firm vegetables such as potatoes. They can be time consuming to prepare but worthwhile for a group; after everyone has had a turn they are thrown away.

Tools you save for printing may not be easy to replace immediately, so it is worth cleaning and storing them for next time. I leave mine to soak for an hour in the sink with plenty of hot water and a little washing up liquid. To save time, I wipe them superficially and place them on newspaper to dry then store them in a plastic container; leaving the lid slightly ajar to avoid mildew growth on any that are not quite dry.

Printing using Recycled Tools

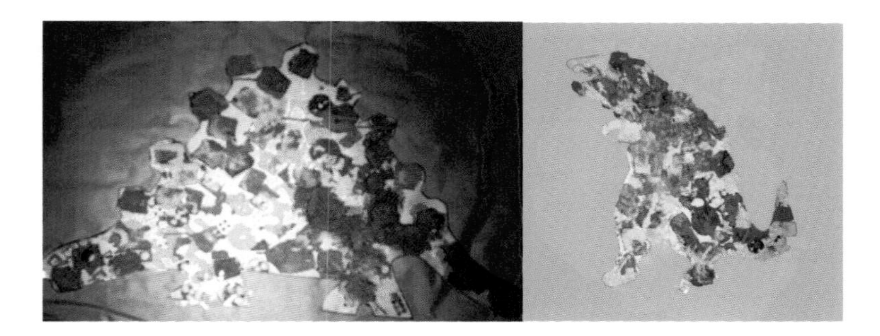

Choose a tool placing one end into a shallow tray of paint; clean plastic supermarket vegetable trays are ideal. Ask your child to grip the other end and make an imprint by pressing the tool down on a sheet of paper. He continues making a number of impressions dunking the object back in the paint as he goes. Draw his attention to how the image is initially bright gradually fading with each successive imprint. Let him continue to print with the other tools then chat about the shapes and textural effects produced by the various objects.

He enjoys making these random prints; as a change from white paper and card he could print on coloured sugar paper, tissue paper, packing paper and even cotton fabric. Much later, giving more thought to where he makes his imprints, he may naturally start to create pattern, e.g. three red bottle top imprints encircling three blue cotton reel imprints.

Comb Printing

Buy combs for printing from toyshops, art shops, educational suppliers, or make your own from stiff card cutting out for the teeth. Apply paint to the paper thickly in dabs for your child to comb, or let him dip the comb into a tray of paint refreshing it as necessary. He can comb the paint over the paper making swirls, lines, curves, circles and even grids if he overlays horizontal and vertical combing. As the paint dries tonal differences become apparent. Point this out to him, 'Why does it happen'. You can explain that the artwork is lighter where teeth have dragged much of the paint away and darker in areas untouched by the comb's teeth. A textural effect, caused by the gaps in the comb, is also achieved, ideal for pictures with blades of grass, waves, animal fur and so on. If he applies the paint thickly he may be able to feel the slightly raised areas of combing.

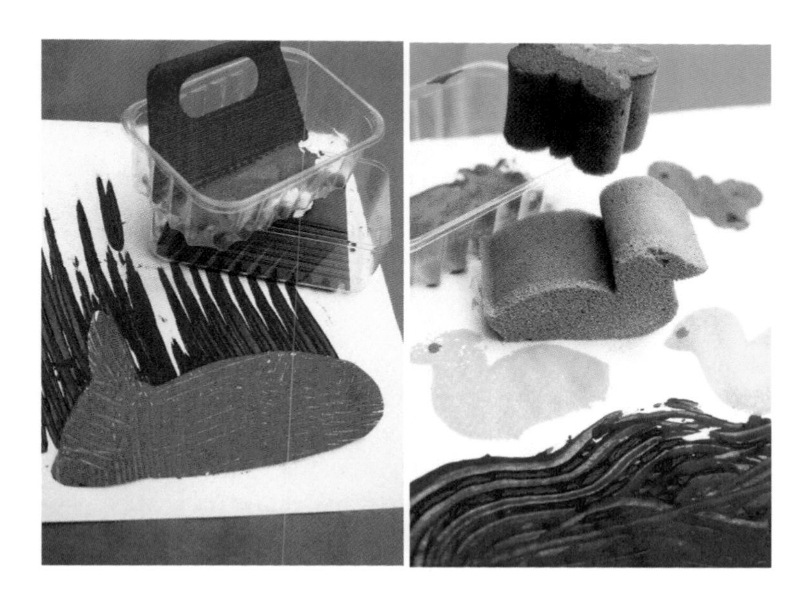

Sponge Printing

Retrieve some foam from your store of printing tools; if you have some natural sponge even better, and cut out a piece substantial enough for your child to grip. Dip one end into a small tray of paint and let your child explore sponge printing with one colour to begin with. Chat with him about the differences in tone, and the fine textural appearance produced by tiny holes in the foam.

Printing with randomly broken sponge or foam is particularly creative but commercial pre-formed foam sets: e.g. transport, animal and geometric shapes can be a novelty and reasonably creative, in conjunction with other materials and techniques or as part of a theme at settings.

Bead Printing

Place a sheet of paper in a clean food tray. Find a small plastic threading ball, or bead from an old necklace, and ask your child to dip it into paint until well covered then transfer it to the tray, which he moves gently backwards, forwards and side to side. The bead rolls around leaving behind interesting trails of paint on the paper.

A SPECIAL OCCASION CARD WITH RED BAUBLE SHAPE SPLATTERED WITH GOLD BEAD PAINT TRAILS.

Hand Printing

Avoid restricting your child, let him explore hand printing on a large scale; use sheets of newspaper - bright coloured paint stands out against the black typeface, wallpaper remnants, packing paper and so on. He paints the palm of his hand with a paintbrush, sponge or presses it flat onto paint soaked foam held in a tray. The latter method, requiring a great deal of paint, is more applicable for settings. He enjoys covering the paper with handprints, working on a floor covered with extra newspaper, and replenishing

his hand with paint as necessary. Over time encourage him to move around the picture, printing from various angles and rotating his hand to create pattern.

Hand printing may naturally lead to finger painting as he sweeps his paint-coated fingers across the paper producing lines, spots, swirls and curves. If you would like to introduce finger painting as a separate activity spread out polythene, an old plastic tablecloth or large sheets of paper, put a dollop of paint, with a little fairy liquid mixed in, on top and let him dig in with his forefinger or fingers. He may return to finger painting on other occasions, e.g. the red spots and stalks on the flowers below could be finger painted, the grass too.

ONE FLOWER SPONGE PRINT AND ONE FLOWER HANDPRINT WITH PAINTED STALK AND LEAVES. WITH A LARGE SHEET OF PAPER YOU CAN CONTINUE PRINTING, CREATING A SPECTACULAR DISPLAY OF MASSED FLOWERS WHICH COULD STAND ALONE OR BE BACKGROUND FOR FURTHER ARTWORK.

Leaf Printing

When out walking let your child scoop up some freshly fallen leaves - from an easily recognised deciduous tree species free of any toxic properties. Check first that the leaves are not contaminated with any excrement, litter, mud etc. On your return, he can help you select the best leaves for printing. Taking one he presses it into a tray containing paint soaked foam; alternatively he paints one side of the leaf with a paintbrush, using less paint. Then he lays the leaf on a sheet of paper pressing down firmly; as he peels it off its imprint is revealed with the network of veins. Vary the paint colour according to the season – see mixed media 'Autumnal Display' at chapter end.

Painting Activities

Shadow Painting

Fold a large sheet of paper in half. Using bright colours your child paints one half. When he is finished help him fold the other half, on top of the painted side, and press down. Let him gently prise the two sides apart to reveal a symmetrical painting. Ask him if both sides look similar and why he thinks that is; give him a mirror to see the symmetry in his face. Fascinated, he enjoys painting more of these seemingly magical pictures.

LARGE SHADOW PAINTED BUTTERFLIES, THE BODIES MADE FROM CARD, LOOK STUNNING WHEN PAINTED AND DISPLAYED EN MASSE.

Blow Painting

PAINT IS BLOWN INTO CONTORTED TWISTY, TONAL SHAPES.

With a paintbrush drop small dabs of paint onto a sheet of paper. Help your child to hold a straw close to the paint while he blows through it, sending the paint off in all directions. Stay with him reminding him to blow, not suck, through the straw. The paint is blown into twig like shapes; ask him how he made that happen.

Bubble Painting

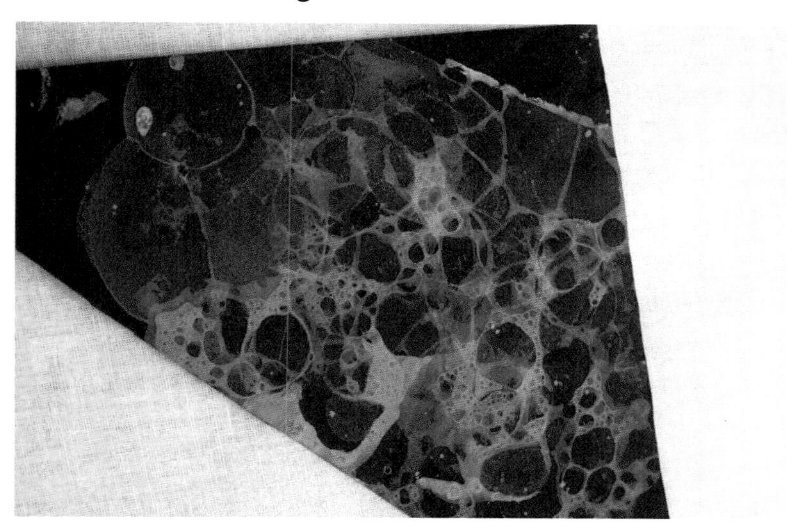

Squeeze a little washing up liquid into a paint pot and stir in some paint. Put a straw into the mixture and show your child how to blow through it; watch to make sure that he blows rather than sucks. As bubbles of paint rise up the pot, catch them by laying a piece of paper down on top. When your child turns the paper over he sees a delicate pattern of circles. Talk about how his blowing disturbs the mixture, pumping in lots of air which creates bubbles.

Marble Painting

You can buy marble paints in small pots; two or three colours are enough, from toyshops, art shops and educational suppliers. Only use under supervision. Also, marble paint contains oil so spills are not easy to remove.

THE ORDINARY FISH SHAPE, CUT FROM THIN WHITE CARD, IS TRANSFORMED INTO SOMETHING EXOTIC BY MARBLE PAINTING. THE EFFECT OF THIS PAINT ON PAPER APPEARS MAGICAL, WITH A TRACERY OF COLOURS AND MOTTLING, NOT UNLIKE THE PATCHES AND VEINING IN MARBLE.

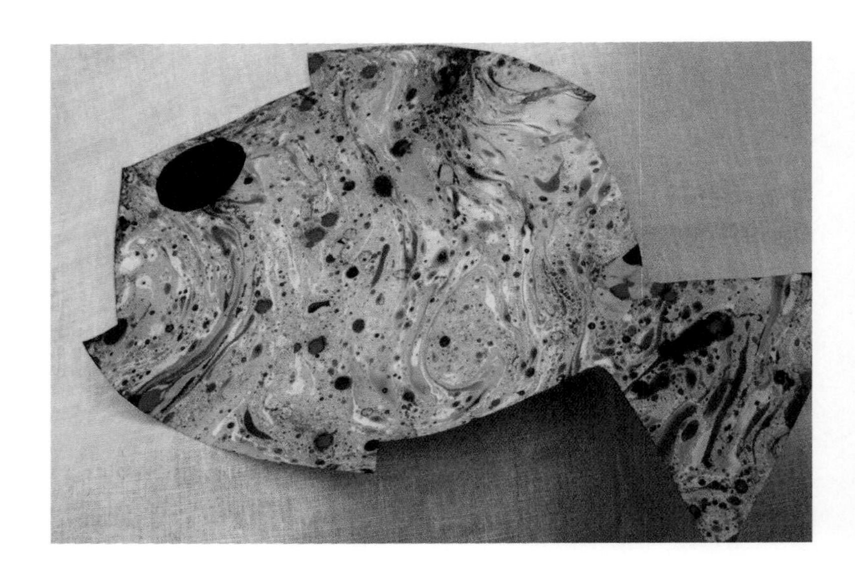

Cover clothes and surfaces; find a large shallow plastic tray, such as a supermarket food tray from your junk-store. Cut about ten sheets of paper slightly smaller than the tray and set aside. Pour water into the tray to a depth of about 1.5cm then dribble over a small amount of paint from each pot.

Let your child gently disperse the paint using an old pencil or spoon. He slides his first sheet of paper onto the floating paint, leaves it for a minute then turns it over to reveal a marbling effect and new colours created by the intermingling of paint. 'Can he see a new colour?' 'What colours combined might have produced it?' The odd spots of orange in the fish image were created when yellow and red combined. He picks up most of the remaining paint with another sheet or two of paper. Point out the particles of paint suspended in the water. Explain that marble paint contains oil, which does not dissolve in water like powder paint, coffee and sugar.

Collage Activities

Visits to museums, farms, zoos and so on: children's story and information books, topics and themes being followed at settings can all be a source of inspiration for collage activities. The choice and application of materials bring texture, depth and pattern to the following pictures.

A SEASONAL COLLAGE PICTURE WITH A LITTLE PAINT OVERLAIN WITH TINSEL, CREPE AND TISSUE PAPERS.

SEASONS: PURPLE AND PINK PATTERNED FABRIC IS USED TO REPRESENT BLOSSOM ON A TREE IN SPRINGTIME.

HERE A BUTTERFLY IS BRIGHT AND FLUTTERY COVERED WITH TRANSLUCENT AND SHINY SPARKLY SWEET WRAPPERS. POINT OUT THE NEW COLOURS AND DEEPER TONES VISIBLE WHERE YOUR CHILD'S COLOURED AND TRANSLUCENT COLLAGE PIECES OVERLAP.

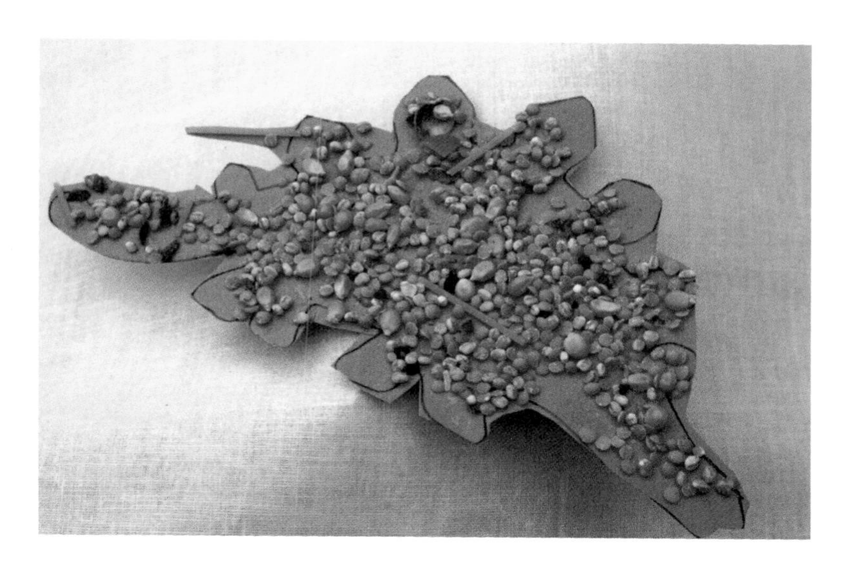

THE DINOSAUR ABOVE IS GIVEN TEXTURE WITH LENTILS, PEARL BARLEY AND VARIOUS OTHER SEEDS AND THE ONE BELOW WITH SANDPAPER AND BRAN.

Mixed Media

It needs some creative lateral thinking, to fit together all the disparate pieces of art in a pleasing display; but the finished result, up on the wall, is truly magical. Inspiration for integrating art media in one picture or display may come from a theme you are working on, a book, nature, a visit, a film; in fact anything that catches the imagination.

Applying 3D materials

THE QUEEN'S SHOULDERS, STAPLED TO THE DISPLAY BOARD, ARE PADDED WITH NEWSPAPER; ENCASED IN GREEN PAPER AND DECORATED WITH OLD NECKLACES. ALSO STAPLED TO THE BOARD IS HER NEWSPAPER PADDED, PINK SPONGE PAINTED FACE, WITH WHITE WOOL HAIR CROWN ATOP AND SPARKLY PAPER FOR FACIAL FEATURES. THE QUEEN OF HEARTS SHE MADE SOME TARTS – OF BAKED SALT DOUGH HERE.

Create the picture directly onto the background paper, or fix pieces of art individually or use a combination of methods. PVA glue is easy to use and can, generally, hold the extra weight of larger 3D materials. The glue held the baked salt-dough tarts in the 'Queen of Hearts' display and the boxes in 'Robots in Space'. To ensure effective adhesion use plenty of glue and position displays horizontally, on the floor or a table, giving them longer to dry, overnight preferably. Notice the shiny glue dribble emanating from the rocket which was stuck on later when the display was in an upright position.

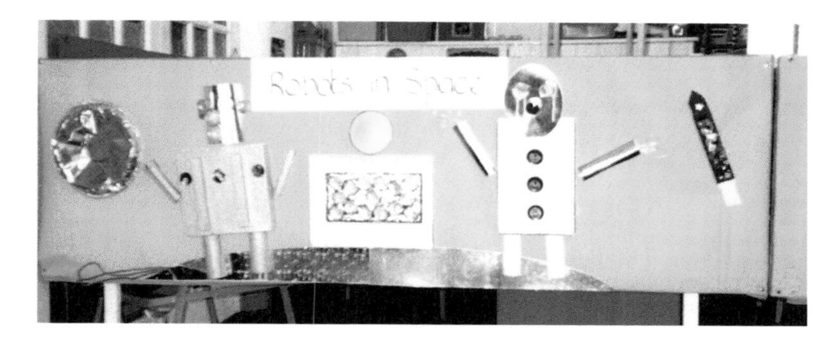

SILVER PAINTED ROBOTS CONSTRUCTED FROM JUNK: BOXES, CARDBOARD TUBES, CHOCOLATE TRAYS AND POLYSTYRENE. SILVER CARD, FLAT OR CURLED, IS USED FOR THE ROBOT S' HEADS AND BUTTONS FOR THEIR DIALS. THEY STAND ON A SPARKLY PLANET CUT FROM GEOMETRIC PATTERNED SILVER CARD WITH ONE ROBOT ATTACHED BY A GREEN LACE.

A MELANGE, INDISTINCTLY HAND PRINTED TREE TRUNKS AND LEAVES WITH COLLAGE SQUIRRELS AND RABBITS DOTTED AROUND IN AN AUTUMNAL DISPLAY.

NB. Learning Outcomes for this chapter are included at the end of Chapter 3.

5

Modelling Materials

Playing with malleable materials such as playdough and soft clay and plasticine, a less pliable more resistant material, is a soothing satisfying experience for your child. Discovering ways to work the different materials is a sociable, as well as a creative, activity. At settings, make time to join the modelling table and at home sit down, when you can, alongside as she plays with the materials. Your interest and chat is encouraging for her.

Preparation

Modelling materials can be messy; use a table with a washable surface and cover the floor, particularly carpet. Protect clothes with painting overalls or let her wear old clothes. To avoid modelling materials being trampled through the home, as soon as she finishes ask her to help you sweep the floor and shake out the covers, which she enjoys. Together clear the tools away, roughly scrape off loose bits then immerse in warm water. Leave to soak long enough to remove the remaining bits effortlessly. Place the tools on newspaper to dry and store in a lidless plastic container, so the air can circulate and finish the drying process.

Chat, asking her, 'why is it easier to clean the tools in warm water?' 'What would happen if we closed the lid on damp tools?'

Storage

Store playdough in a plastic food box in the fridge or somewhere cool; it should keep fresh for a number of weeks, the salt acts as a preservative. To keep the playdough extra soft you could cover it in clingfilm first – only let your child handle clingfilm under supervision for safety reasons. If it feels sticky when unwrapped just sprinkle a dusting of flour on the dough for your child to work in. Cover clay in a wet cloth and store tightly in plastic to prevent it drying out. Explain that the air takes the moisture from the clay, into the atmosphere, if it is unwrapped. Plasticine tends not to dry out and is usually fine stored in plastic tubs.

BEN WRAPS THE PLAYDOUGH IN CLINGFILM BEFORE STORING.

Playdough

Playdough contains the basic ingredients flour, salt and water and is sometimes referred to as saltdough. Explain that the salt preserves the dough keeping it fresh. Commercial play dough can be bought in toyshops, craft shops and some stationers and lasts well if placed back in the tub after use. It is easy cheap and convenient to make your own playdough, in small quantities for home use, larger for settings. Your child also has the opportunity to help you mix the ingredients and knead them to a pliable, ready to use, dough.

Playdough Recipe

KITCHEN UTENSILS

Mug or cup
Large mixing bowl
Large spoon

BEN POURS ½ MUG OF WATER INTO THE FLOUR AND SALT MIXTURE THEN USES A WOODEN SPOON TO MIX THE INGREDIENTS TOGETHER.

INGREDIENTS	MEASUREMENTS	
	HOME	GROUP
Plain flour	1 cup	2 cups
Salt	½ cup	1 cup
Water	½ cup	1 cup
Cooking oil	½ teaspoon	1 teaspoon
Food colour (optional)	½ teaspoon	1 teaspoon

Measure the flour and salt into the bowl then roughly stir together. Before pouring the water in add food colour to it, if required. Then add the oil and stir for a few minutes until the ingredients are mixed in. Keeping the dough in the bowl, pummel it for about five minutes, turning it frequently. During this time the water continues absorbing the other ingredients eventually forming a pliable ball of dough.

Coloured Playdough

Make the first batches of dough neutral so your child can concentrate on the physical properties of the dough without the distraction of colour. Later, when you introduce colour fresh interest is generated in the activity. Settings could change playdough colour on a rotational basis or according to a current theme; retaining children's keenness to continue exploring and being creative with dough.

Using the measurements above, I find yellow, green and red food colours produce brightly coloured playdough; cochineal comes out pink rather than red and blue and black colours tend to produce dingy looking dough. Try increasing the measure to achieve a brighter result. Experiment with other food colours; there are plenty available in supermarkets, independent grocers and delis.

Exploring Modelling Materials

This is an opportunity to pose questions and chat about her discoveries. Occasionally divide the material between you both; she likes to see you handling it too. You can hang back, letting her do the major experimenting. At settings she notices how other children are modelling their material and tries copying, which is a natural part of the learning process for her. Over time she begins to understand how each type of modelling material performs and compares, e.g. plasticine held up in the air is rigid; playdough is loose and floppy.

BEN HOLDS AN ELONGATED PIECE OF PLAYDOUGH IN THE AIR. HE DISCOVERS IT IS MUCH MORE ELASTIC THAN PLASTICINE AND SOON FALLS APART.

She can:

- Roll, squeeze, squash, tear, flatten and shape the modelling material
- Elongate/stretch it and hold it in the air
- Press it with her palms backwards and forwards into a worm like shape
- Pull it apart, into large and small pieces and return it to a ball again
- Flatten it by pressing down heavily

ROLLING PLASTICINE

- Imprint the material by pressing in fingers, palm, heel or sides of her hand
- Roll the lump of material round and round on the table making rudimentary ball shapes of various sizes
- Roll a lump of material (she may have noticed others doing this) between her palms achieving a smooth ball-shape finish (this requires a degree of physical co-ordination and experience)
- Cover plates and line bowls (from her toy dinner service) with modelling material she has flattened
- Blend different coloured play dough or different coloured plasticine creating new colours and marbling effects

ENJOYING SOFT CLAY AT A POTTERY BARN.

Pretend Food and Pretend Play

Many of the shapes she makes, as she explores modelling materials, remind her of food. They become part of imaginative play as she feeds her toys and you; it might be wise to restrict play to an easily cleaned area. Later, she may intentionally make dough food, e.g. chips and sausages, pancakes and pizzas, peas, cherries and scoops of ice cream. She enjoys filling play pots and pans with pretend food, cooking it then setting it on plates. She may sometimes complete the arrangement with cutlery and cups inviting visitors to her home, shop or café for refreshments.

Using Tools with Modelling Materials

Introduce tools gradually; she discovers what she can achieve working the material with a particular tool or set of tools, before moving on to others.

USING A BRUSH TO DIP INTO THE SLIP – A MIX OF WATER AND CLAY WHICH KEEPS THE CLAY MOIST.

WORKING WITH TOOLS: SQUEEZING DOUGH INTO THIN STRIPS THROUGH A GARLIC CRUSHER, CHOPPING IT INTO BITS WITH PLASTIC KNIVES, STRETCHING IT OUT WITH A ROLLING PIN, CUTTING SHAPES WITH PASTRY CUTTERS.

Squeezing

Encourage your child to squeeze a lump of dough, hard in her fist, then watch it escape between her fingers. For a fascinating, seemingly magical, effect place a small ball of dough in a garlic crusher then help her squeeze the handle; she sees the dough forced through the holes and transformed into long thin or short stubby strips. After this trick I always put the garlic crusher straight into warm water, garlic is difficult enough to dislodge; if left, dough is almost impossible. Let her also try pressing dough into an old sieve or tea strainer to see it oozing out the other side.

Slicing the Modelling Materials

Once she realises that toy plastic knives cut through modelling materials, easily and neatly, she is off chopping materials into myriad pieces. Point out how smooth the cut surface is; compared to the rough edges left when she separates materials by hand. Take her to a supermarket deli counter or cheese shop, to see the assistant cut a triangle of cheese smoothly with a wire cutter. For a similar effect at home, use an egg slicer, to cut hard-boiled eggs even a ball of dough.

Rolling the Modelling Materials

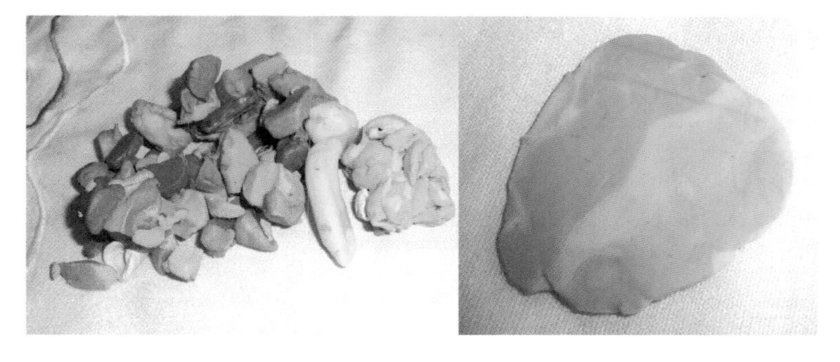

CHOPPED PLASTICINE PRETEND FOOD, ARRANGED IN A COLOURFUL PILE, AND BLUE AND YELLOW PLASTICINE BLENDED FLATTENED AND ROLLED UNTIL SMOOTH.

So far your child has applied hand pressure alone to flatten modelling materials. Using a junior rolling pin, she discovers materials not only stretch much further but are also flatter and smoother. Engage her in conversation, encouraging her to experiment. 'Which material is the hardest to roll out, dough, plasticine or clay? Lift up the rolled out materials. Which one stretches the most? Which is the least likely to collapse?'

Cutting Shapes

'Could you line this plastic bowl with rolled out modelling material?' 'Is the piece big enough, will you have to add some more or chop some away?' 'What tools can you use to cut out shapes?' As well as general shape cutters others can be bought to fit themes, such as transport and animals cutters. Has she any other suggestions e.g. pan lids from her dinner service for cutting circle shapes. Perhaps she could roll out pastry for pies and biscuits using another set of utensils, of course.

Imprinting

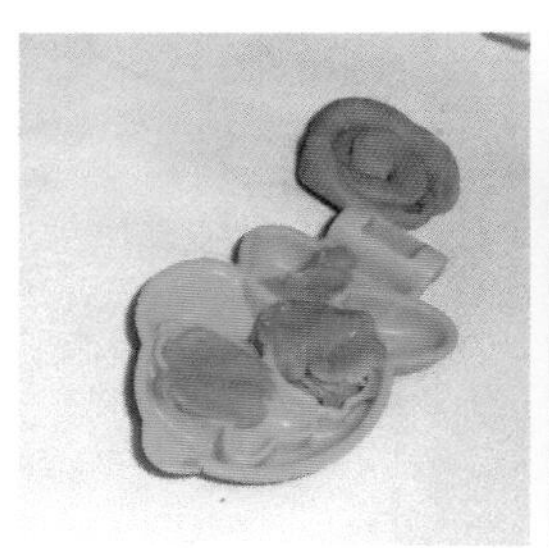

A RELIEF DESIGN IS REVEALED WHEN THE PLASTICINE IS REMOVED FROM THE MOULD AND A LACY PATTERN IS REVEALED WHEN THE PLASTIC DOYLEY IS LIFTED.

Create relief and pattern by imprinting modelling materials. A variety of tools are suitable, such as, cotton reels, bottle tops and combs from your printing store, plastic forks, animal shapes and interlocking bricks from the play area and utensils such as biscuit and jelly moulds, potato masher and sieves. Check the objects you select are not broken or damaged and introduce a few at a time. Help her to grip the tool safely particularly any adult sized kitchen tools. Educational suppliers have a range of imprinting and embossing tools for use with modelling materials and damp sand.

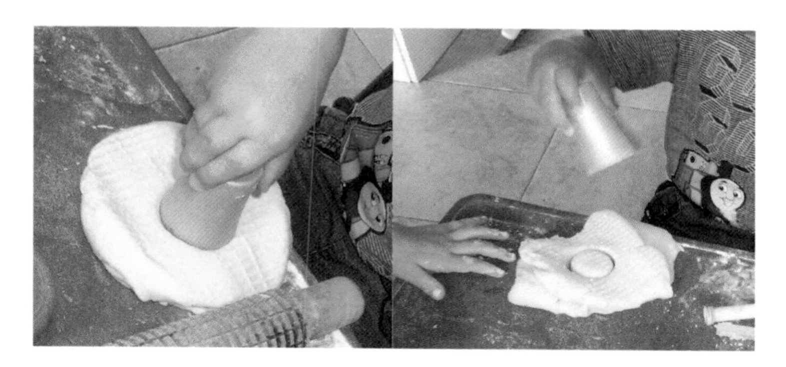

Ask her to touch the imprints she makes, 'What do they feel like?' Look at the imprinting tools together, 'What caused these bumps?' Explain that the raised areas appear, when she presses the tool down forcing modelling material through spaces and holes and into the recesses of moulds. After a while, she might explore imprinting to create pattern, pictures or tell a story.

RELIEF CREATED HERE BY IMPRINTING WITH A TOY FORK, SHAPES, GLUE STICK, COTTON REEL AND BOTTLE TOPS.

Embellishing

Oddments, natural and everyday, worked into modelling materials can result in some weird and wonderful creations. Together, pick bits from your collage store, such as shells, pebbles, pasta shapes, acorns and buttons. To begin with, she may explore by pressing the object into a lump of modelling material until completely buried, like an old three-penny piece in a Xmas pudding. She may apply items randomly, as surface decoration, to see how they appear. Later, with a purpose in mind, she could draw what she hopes to achieve, she may seek out particular items as embellishment.

Baking Play/Salt Dough for Pretend Play

BAKED HARD FOR PRETEND PLAY: SALT DOUGH PIZZA, CHERRY BUNS, JAM TARTS AND CHAPPATIS.

Using playdough food in imaginative play often entails restricting play to an easily cleaned area. If the pretend food is baked until hard she can play with it almost anywhere, an asset, particularly for settings (Do not bake commercial playdough unless the manufacturer says otherwise). I use a fresh batch of playdough but bake it to rather haphazard timings so I recommend you find baking instructions for salt dough online. Search for 'salt dough craft', the craft is popular and includes ingredients for the dough as well as baking instructions.

Colourful breakfast food, bacon rashers, fried eggs, sausages, tomatoes and chips, is ideal for pretend play in the home or café. Mould the dough into substantial pieces of food, e.g. thick rashers of bacon, they are more satisfying to handle and less likely to get lost.

Hard baked pretend food appears more realistic when painted, normal powder paints are perfectly adequate. She can paint the cooled food and when dry you may be able to apply a protective finish with a high quality non-toxic varnish, suitable for children. As children sometimes lick the food check current health and safety guidelines, if in doubt do not use varnish or paint. It is a source of pride for her, to think that she has created toys she can use in pretend play.

Making a Clay Coil Pot

A flattened piece of clay forms the pot base and your child rolls out thin sausages winding them around the base. She brushes the sausages with slip which sticks them together and then she smoothes them so they are less sausage-like. If she is making the coil pot at a pottery barn they normally fire it and allow her to return to paint it; the process may take a few weeks. Settings could perhaps use a local pottery's kiln or try a product called Newclay which air dries to a non-brittle finish.

Learning Outcomes

Science

- Stirs combining water, flour, gritty salt and food colour
- Observes dry loose ingredients absorbing liquids
- Pummels dough until smooth and pliable notices food colour blending into and colouring the dough as she pummels
- Understands warm soapy water loosens dough from tools
- Realises tools need air to dry (that air takes moisture into atmosphere – vapour) left damp they may go mouldy
- Maintains the dough sprinkling flour on sticky dough and kneading until smooth again
- Covers clay with wet cloth and plastic to maintain softness

- Handling the materials is a satisfying sensory experience
- Discovers she can roll, squeeze, squash, tear, flatten, stretch, press, pull apart, imprint and shape the modelling materials
- Compares the materials, finds playdough and clay are more pliable than plasticine
- Utilises a variety of tools to slice, roll out, squeeze, imprint and embellish the modelling material
- Observes effects on modelling materials using hands and tools, e.g. smooth cut with tool, rough when pulled apart
- Utilises tools creating a range of effects and relief patterns
- Squeezes malleable materials through fine holes into strips
- Imprints and feels the projections and indentations created
- Notices soft material becomes rock hard when baked or fired

Language, Personal and World Around

- Takes inspiration from experience, outdoors and stories
- Joins in preparation maintenance and cleaning of materials
- Finds playing with modelling materials a relaxing activity conducive to conversation
- Socialises with other children as she works the materials
- Learns new vocabulary as you describe what is happening

Creativity

- Experiments freely with malleable dough and clay
- Works plasticine within its less flexible constraints
- Transforms dough into shapes of her own choosing using both hands and tools
- Chooses vivid plasticine colours and blends them together
- Moulds materials into something: coil pot, pretend food
- Extends imaginative play possibilities with dough play food
- Makes pretend dough food, has it baked, then paints it
- Embellishes dough with natural materials

Mathematics and Fine Physical Skills

- Appreciates as she works the materials how their physical properties change from their original form to something new
- Cuts shapes out of flattened dough often counting in the process
- Imprints using a range of tools frequently creating patterns
- Lines toy dinner plates and bowls with dough (area)
- Presses objects into dough until hidden, if necessary adding more dough (measurement – area)
- Realises the quantity of dough remains the same whether it is in one lump or broken into bits - the dough is conserved
- Sculpts dough into 3D shapes, e.g. ball and worm shapes, of various sizes
- Develops dexterity and hand eye co-ordination as she manipulates dough with hands and tools

Special Needs

All learning outcomes in chapters 5, 6, 7, 8 may apply; the learning outcomes below may be particularly appropriate.

- Experiments freely with malleable dough and clay, finds handling the materials a satisfying sensory experience
- Discovers can roll, squeeze, squash, tear, flatten, stretch, press, pull apart, imprint, blend, shape modelling materials
- Transforms dough using both hands and tools; uses the latter to slice, roll, squeeze, imprint and embellish the materials.
- Works, the less pliable, vivid plasticine blending their colours
- Socialises with other children as she works the materials
- Joins in imaginative play with others, gains in confidence as interacts in the often complex structures of imaginary play
- Expresses feelings of annoyance, frustration and tenderness, without repercussions, when playing with toys like dolls
- Co-operates sharing toys and props, settles disagreements, and reaches decisions with others to help play along

6

Imaginative Play

Pretend play is an essential part of growing up and generally your child plays imaginatively quite naturally, whether on his own or with others. As he plays he tries things out, tests what he knows, making sense of the world. He may take on particular roles such as parent, patient, fire fighter, or play may be very energetic and spontaneous with less emphasis on roles. During small world imaginative play, described in 'Book 3', your child plays, often on his own, with toys which are miniature versions of real things such as cars, garage, dolls house, figures.

Of course it is important for your child, however socially inclined, to have the opportunity to play with others, as well as on his own. He may play confidently with others from early on. On the other hand, he may play alongside but independently from other children, later on exchanging toys and snippets of conversation. Eventually, however tentatively, he begins to take part in pretend play with other children, perhaps even chatting and organising props and roles with them. Suggestions in this chapter, and the following two chapters, show how to set up the framework for play, choosing themes, toys and props, and how you can enthuse children by occasionally joining in their play.

Dressing Up Clothes

REAL CLOTHES AND ACCESSORIES CAREFULLY SELECTED, OFFER GREAT SCOPE FOR DRESSING UP: PICTURED HERE A RICHARD THE LIONHEART TABARD, (PREVIOUSLY USED IN A PANTO), CAMOUFLAGE SCARF, FLORAL DRESS (SHORTENED FOR SAFETY REASONS), TWO HATS DRAPED WITH SCARVES, SILK EMBROIDERED HANDBAG AND WHITE FRINGED WRAP.

Wearing dressing up clothes, accessories and hats adds another dimension to imaginative play, helping your child to feel in character. Collect as many real clothes as possible, the sheer variety of materials cannot be matched by commercial dressing up clothes, nor their potential in a wider range of pretend play situations. Carry out necessary alterations to your dressing up clothes, donations and charity shop finds.

Fine and Fancy

Collect an assortment of fancy, glittery, rich dressing up clothes, hats and accessories for children to select unique combinations. Raid your wardrobe, ask family and friends for anything fitting this description, that they are thinking of throwing out anyway; e.g. bridesmaid dresses, camouflage army jackets, ballet tutus, faux fur wraps, all of which should, preferably, fit easily over children's own clothes. Avoid the possibility of your child tripping up, by trimming hems and sleeves; use pinking shears to save time although sewn hems withstand wear better at settings.

A FRINGED BOLERO AND SKIRT CUT FROM A SUEDE SKIRT; CRAFT FEATHERS ATTACHED TO ELASTIC FOR A HEADBAND.

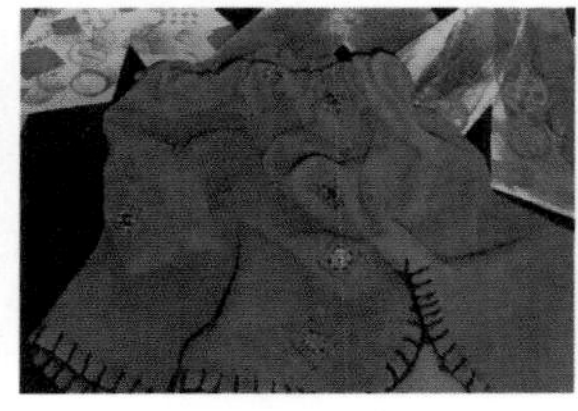

CROWNS FROM A BEEFBURGER CHAIN EMBELLISHED WITH COSTUME JEWELLERY, LUSTROUS SATIN CAPES (FIXED AT THE FRONT WITH EASY TO PULL APART VELCRO) AND A MIRROR TO SEE HOW THEY LOOK.

Role Play Clothes and Hats

Wearing a reflective vest and a construction worker's safety hat, he is transported to the role of builder, maintenance worker; any job where visibility is paramount. Costumes and hats produced for children's imaginative play particularly worth purchasing, are those which reflect jobs, e.g. nurse and police officer uniforms. Ordinary grown-up style clothes such as waistcoats, gilets, jackets, clip-on ties, short sleeve shirts, help your child imagine himself in the role of parent/carer and office worker.

HELMETS AND HEADGEAR THAT DENOTE THE ROLE OF THE WEARER ARE REALISTIC, INEXPENSIVE AND EASY TO PUT ON; HE IMMEDIATELY FEELS IN CHARACTER. HATS RELATED TO NO PARTICULAR ROLE ARE POPULAR TOO; LARGE FLOPPY, COLOURFUL HATS, USED ONCE OR TWICE FOR WEDDINGS THEN DISCARDED ARE CHEAP TO BUY FROM CHARITY SHOPS, YOU CAN ADD ADORNMENTS SUCH AS FLOWERS AND FRUIT OR WIND SILK SCARVES AROUND THE BRIM.

Multicultural Clothes

If you enjoy sewing ask friends and family going to Asia on holiday or business to purchase a length of exotic fabric or buy locally at Indian clothes shops. Make up into traditional Asian wear, for pretend play, looking first at pictures for inspiration. Roughly draw a simple shift design on newspaper, fitting it against your child and making alterations, before cutting the material. Sew edges to prevent fraying and make it easy for your child to take on and off by using velcro fixings. For traditional male dress you could cut the collar off an older boy's white shirt then button it up, on your child, back to front.

SETTINGS CAN PURCHASE GOOD PLAY CLOTHES DEPICTING OTHER CULTURES FROM SPECIALIST SUPPLIERS. THE ONE HERE COMPRISES ASIAN LADY'S SKIRT, BLOUSE AND LENGTH OF LONG WIDE MATCHING FABRIC FOR DRAPING.

ASIAN CLOTHES CAN BE VIBRANTLY COLOURED AND DECORATED, LIKE THESE TWO CHINESE EMBROIDERED TOPS, FOR AN ADULT AND CHILD.

Buying Dressing up Clothes

Apart from simple tabards and shifts, repairs and alterations, shortening hems and sleeves, there is no need to make dressing up clothes. They are widely available and can be purchased inexpensively, use them to supplement your own collection. Educational suppliers offer a range with easy fixings and extra material allowance to go easily over the top of children's own clothes. Superhero and character costumes based on television programmes and films have limited play value and are not really suitable for settings. With a narrow range of play possibilities, they can induce passivity in the wearer. In contrast, a costume layered up to fit his requirements, gives him ownership and scope for creative and imaginative play.

THE FAIRY PRINCESS HERE ENJOYS DANCING IN THIS COSTUME.

Accessories

Accumulate accessories; old scarves (for safety reasons worn around the waist - perhaps flamboyantly for pirates), shawls, gloves, clip-on ties, hats, belts, handbags, bracelets, purses and wallets - fill the latter two with shiny penny and half penny coins. Hunt accessories out at charity shops and around the home. Clean and regularly check them, in fact all dressing up clothes, and repair or throw away any unsafe items. Where accessories are used, watch the play at all times; for safety reasons.

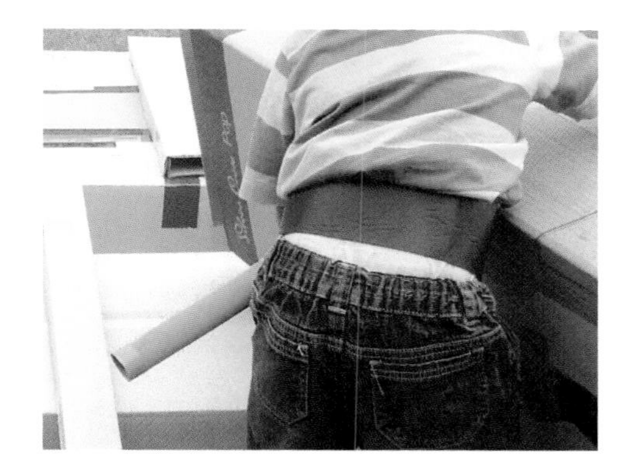

JOHNSON REJECTED THE PIRATE DRESSING UP CLOTHES ON OFFER. INSTEAD HE SELECTED THE BELT AND PAINTED CARDBOARD TELESCOPE. CHILDREN WHO DISLIKE DRESSING UP ARE OFTEN HAPPY TO DON ACCESSORIES AND HATS AND HELMETS; THEY IMMEDIATELY FEEL IN CHARACTER.

At home, empty, scrupulously clean, lipsticks and compacts, stored in cosmetic bags add an authentic touch to imaginative role play. Settings probably preclude their use for hygiene reasons. I think there is an important distinction between real make up labelled and sold to the pre-school age group and the use of an adult's empty compacts for imaginative play. Children instinctively understand that the latter are for grown-ups and they are playing a role when they use them.

Storage and Display

Ideally, dressing up clothes should be hung where children can see and reach them, particularly at settings. Having them visible and accessible is appealing - hanging from wall pegs, a securely attached rail or a purpose made unit. Accessories such as handbags and hats look attractive draped from pegs or arranged on shelves. Jewellery stands out displayed in tiers on cardboard cake stands. If it is impractical to have everything on show, display a couple of items and tempt further investigation by packing the rest into ancient hatboxes, suitcases, hampers or baskets.

HERE CHILDREN CAN CHOOSE FROM THE CLOTHES HANGING UP THEN RUMMAGE AROUND IN THE BOX BELOW TO SELECT ACCESSORIES.

Energetic Imaginative Play

Jumping climbing and running around is all part of energetic spontaneous, imaginative play. In keeping with the informality of the play children may need little involvement from you, apart perhaps from initial setting up, checking play remains safe, and providing additional props and suggestions if play is flagging or getting too noisy. Outdoors is ideal for energetic imaginative play and indoors at settings with a spacious room or hall allowing for free movement. Safety Assessments should be carried out for all features referred to in this section.

Green Outdoor Areas

GREEN AREAS, WITH SHRUBS AND TREES, OFFER SECRET PLACES, UNDERGROWTH TO CRAWL THROUGH AND MOUNDS AND HILLS AS LOOKOUTS.

While some hard surfaced areas outside are necessary for children's play, including imaginative play, keeping or creating as much green as possible, grass, plants, bushes and trees provides a rich framework for active imaginative play. Into this environment could go a section of tree trunk, laid horizontally, for children to crawl and balance along to climb and to spring from. Undergrowth to plot and hide in, a tunnel to creep and crawl through and mounds, boulders, slopes to view things from.

Props

Props need only be an approximation of what he requires; his imagination does the rest. Plastic hoops, whistle and a section of garden hose can trigger play. A hose can put out a fire, fill vehicles with petrol and tyres with air, a whistle blown akin to a siren announces ambulance police car and fire engine. He can pick out a few hats, helmets, clothes and accessories linked to the play theme. Of course, keep a constant eye on children, supervising active informal pretend play closely.

BOATS AND SHIPS

USE AN OLD WOODEN BOAT, LIKE THIS, AS A RESOURCE WITH SEATS INTACT BOUGHT OR BEGGED; CHECKED FOR SPLINTERS AND ROT THEN REPAIRED, PAINTED AND FIXED SECURELY IN PLACE. POSITIONED SAFELY OUTDOORS IT MEANS LOTS OF CLIMBING IN AND OUT, MOVING AROUND, BALANCING ON DECK AND IT CAN BE TURNED INTO A PIRATE BOAT, FISHING BOAT, HOUSEBOAT AND FERRY BOAT.

Take advice about renovating a boat and securing it fast. Harness enthusiasm by reading a story to your child and his friends about life on board a pirate ship, for example and create some props. Folded newspaper pirate hats painted with skull and crossbones, a cardboard tube mast strapped securely in the bow, an old sheet for sails and a pirate flag to finish it off.

RECYCLED BOXES

RECYCLE STRONG CARDBOARD BOXES AND TUBES FOR ACTIVE IMAGINATIVE PLAY. TRANSFORM THEM INTO VEHICLES, BOATS, PLANES, ROCKETS, TRAINS AND HIDEY-HOLES. IF YOU WISH, EMBELLISH THESE TEMPORARY PROPS. FOR EXAMPLE, FOR A VEHICLE PAINT ON CAR WHEELS AND USE A HOOP AS A STEERING WHEEL.

JOHNSON CARRIES, PULLS, LIFTS AND MANOEUVRES LARGE CARDBOARD TUBES AND BOXES INTO POSITION. HIS TELESCOPE, A PAINTED CARDBOARD TUBE, IS PUSHED INTO A WIDE BELT FROM DRESSING UP. THE PIRATE SHIPS' DECKS ARE FIRM ENOUGH FOR CHILDREN TO SIT ON, AS THEY LOOK OUT FOR TREASURE AND COUNT THEIR BOOTY.

Dens: Hiding Places

A den might be any partially enclosed space for your child and other children to shelter and take refuge from imaginary enemies, after foraging for food, checking the landscape and mounting campaigns. Dens are generally temporary structures, hiding places: one might be built with branches and twigs in a woodland clearing, another indoors under a table and yet another in a gap between furniture, a draped throw as roof.

A rustic outdoor den may be made, with your help, by intertwining twigs or camouflage material into the lower branches of trees and large shrubs. I remember, as a slightly older child, flattening muddy lumps of earth to make pies, laying them on tree trunk tables, in a makeshift home - a gap in the wood. Make temporary indoor and garden dens with blankets, bedspreads and curtains; one spread over a table nearly reaching the ground makes a simple den. Dens are more fun outside but are useful inside during winter and in bad weather.

Tents

An alternative during the summer months, although not as creative as a home-made den, is a tent; avoid those emblazoned with motifs and pictures, they can be too restrictive. Look for a first proper tent, in an interesting shape, such as an igloo tent, with a large opening flap, or a sun protection tent. They are generally single or dual coloured and can be customised to suit the play theme. Pre-school children are sociable, although they enjoy hiding for a short period, they do not like feeling cut off from you or the rest of the group. A den or tent with an open feel avoids this and also allows children to rush in and out easily.

7

Imaginative Home Play

Taking on parental, baby and other family roles is a natural feature of imaginative home play. A home area is essential at settings and easy to achieve at home. Make sure children have enough room to carry out tasks such as making meals, tidying away and caring for baby. Home play may shift, within the constraints of the building, away from the main structure, to other rooms and even the outside area, as a picnic is arranged or a pram, with baby doll tucked up inside, is pushed to the shops.

Your child may take baby doll, or similar toy, around with her everywhere, chatting to it caring for it then suddenly losing interest dropping it – all part and parcel of home play. This type of play is sociable and at home is often best played near you. She engages in home play on her own and with others; joining in with others her play experience broadens. After initial setting up, you may find children need little involvement from you. Play progresses, they have fresh ideas and adjustments are made. As with all play, be ready to offer encouragement, checking play remains safe and intervening if children are unable to resolve disagreements.

Home Area Layout

Traditional Structure

THIS TYPE OF PERMANENT FIXED WOODEN PLAY HOME, WITH SHELVING, IS PRIMARILY USED AT SETTINGS. TO MAXIMISE SPACE FOR CARRYING OUT KITCHEN TASKS, DRESSING UP CLOTHES, TABLE AND COT ARE KEPT OUTSIDE THE STRUCTURE. THIS HOME GIVES CHILDREN A DEGREE OF PRIVACY AND ALLOWS YOU TO OBSERVE WHAT IS GOING ON.

Kitchen Centres

Toy kitchen centres, for use at home, come in plastic or wood, are visually appealing, equipped with storage space (kitchenware usually sold separately), hob, oven, sink and sometimes a dishwasher and fridge. The centres are smaller and lower in height than educational units used at settings. Although your child may tower over the unit after a year, it is still useable; children unconsciously make an allowance during play. An additional surface is usually needed to carry out kitchen tasks.

Adaptable Structures

A flexible arrangement for settings is the purchase, from education suppliers, of wooden modular panels which can be fixed together to form a home area and when required reconfigured for other layouts. Settings buying individual wooden kitchen units e.g. sink or cooker unit can use these to delineate the home area.

A FLEXIBLE STRUCTURE CAN BE CREATED AT HOME. HERE OCCASIONAL TABLES COVERED IN BRIGHT FABRIC PROJECT FROM THE WALL CREATING A U SHAPE HOME AREA. EQUIPMENT IS LAID OUT FOR CARRYING OUT KITCHEN TASKS AND DOLLS ARE ARRANGED TO FEED AND CARE FOR. ON THE FLOOR A RUG SEPARATES THE HOME CORNER FROM THE REST OF THE ROOM.

A temporary home can be easily moved elsewhere (including outdoors) and the space increased to allow for more children and extended play. I think it is important for settings and desirable at home to avoid a duplication of the inside, why erect a 'cute' roofed plastic house in valuable outside space when the inside home area meets needs, and more effectively.

Equipping the Home Area

THIS LIFE LIKE BABY DOLL HAS A SOFT BODY AND SPONGEABLE FACE AND LIMBS. THE VINYL DOLL CAN BE BATHED AND HAS MOVEABLE HEAD AND LIMBS.

Source baby and toddler dolls. Grown up style dolls (marketed for three year olds and up) may shorten childhood, pushing children on to another stage, depriving them of pretend home play where they take on parental roles. Pushing the doll's pram to the play shop, walking the doll around the garden, cuddling the doll when it is upset are physical activities too; play involving grown up dolls is essentially sedentary.

CHILDREN ENJOY USING DRAINING BOARDS; ALTHOUGH NOT SUCH A COMMON FEATURE NOW THEY LINK YOUR CHILD WITH THE PAST.

Toys and Equipment

- Doll with clothes, cot or carrier and blankets/ bedding
- Special needs accessories for dolls, e.g. wheelchair, a walker with bag, spectacles and hearing aids, can be purchased from educational suppliers
- Dinner/tea service, cutlery set and tray
- Asian cooking utensils e.g. wok and dinner service
- Hob oven unit, pan, casserole and cooking utensils
- Combined hob oven/microwave table top unit
- Children's table and chairs (ironing, serving meals, eating)
- Soft toys in lieu of people (visitors, family and friends)
- Two telephones (to hold conversations)
- Bowl, iron (housework)

Hob oven units are space saving, inexpensive, adaptable and perfectly suitable for the home area. Even a simple hob is enough to stimulate home play. This one, with painted red hotplates and yellow dials on smooth plywood, was originally a board from a toy baking set. See it in the photo (Adaptable Structures) where it sits on a pretend work surface - low height furniture covered with a folded tablecloth.

Play Food

Children love to make and use play dough food in the home area; it is satisfyingly malleable. Imagine the busyness of it all as it is prepared, distributed among the pans, cooked, served on plates and bowls then finally presented at table.

SOFT YELLOW AND GREEN PLAYDOUGH FOOD (CONTAINS HIGH PERCENTAGE OF SALT AS A PRESERVATIVE) AND BAKED PLAYDOUGH PAINTED DEEP PAN PIZZAS, BUNS, CHAPPATIS AND JAM TARTS.

Unfortunately, it tends to get trodden onto the floor so at home it is sensible to keep its use to uncarpeted areas. Even then little feet may tread bits through to other rooms, so as a precaution provide plain dough rather than coloured, to avoid food dye being ground into carpets and rugs. Let him play with the coloured dough outside during the summer months. An alternative is to bake dough food; see chapter five modelling materials for playdough recipe and ideas for hard baked playdough food.

AUTHENTIC LOOKING PLASTIC TOY FOOD IS POPULAR WITH CHILDREN. FRUIT AND VEGETABLES I FIND ARE SUCCESSFUL, THEY ARE COLOURFUL AND COME IN A RANGE OF SHAPES, SIZES AND TYPES, ALSO ICE CREAM CONES AND EGGS – USE REAL EGGBOXES. TOY PLASTIC FOOD SHOULD BE STRONG ENOUGH, PARTICULARLY FOR GROUP USE, NOT TO DENT WHEN A BITE IS ATTEMPTED.

Props

SUCTION HOOKS FIXED TO A PLAY HOME WALL FOR DUSTERS, TOWELS AND CLOTHS AND A CARDBOARD WALL CLOCK WITH PLASTIC MOVEABLE HANDS.

From your cupboards:

- Dishcloth, duster, small towel/tea towel, dustpan and brush,
- Old undamaged baby toys, feeding bottle and cup/beaker,
- Pencil, notepaper (clock, diary), (for safety ensure that pencils are put down after use not carried around)
- Dressing up clothes
- Bell (visitor doorbell)
- Other items as they crop up or occur to you

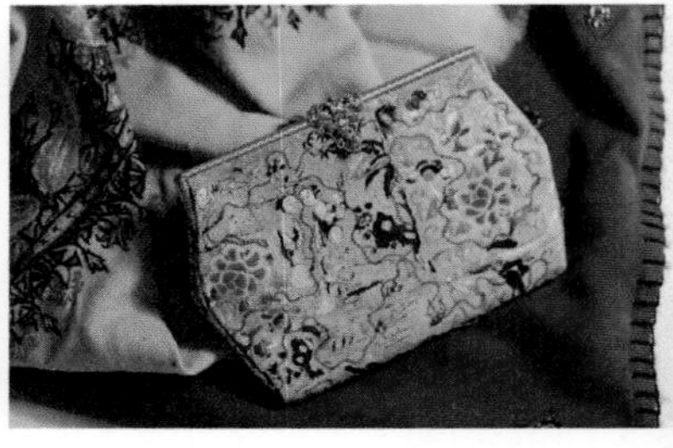

A CHINESE STYLE BAG, EMBROIDERED TEXTILES AND A GENERAL PURPOSE MELAMINE ASIAN DINNER SERVICE. USE IN HOME PLAY WITH EMPTY PACKETS OF RICE, NOODLES, AND CREAMED COCONUT DEPICTING TRADITIONAL ASIAN SCENES AND WRITING. TOY PLASTIC FRUIT FROM AROUND THE WORLD IS AVAILABLE THROUGH EDUCATIONAL SUPPLIERS.

Extending Home Play

Extended home play may happen spontaneously, for example children deciding a fire has started and calling the emergency services out. It may arise after encouraging them to discuss ideas. Sometimes, after talking on a theme, you may initiate play by bringing toys and props together. If any children are worried about a forthcoming visit, for example, to the dentist, or moving house you can alleviate anxiety by setting up a suitable framework - dental surgery with waiting room and boxes for packing home contents and a car with trailer for removals.

Hospital/Medical Centre

Children decide the baby is ill and needs to visit the surgery; they allocate the roles of doctor, nurse, baby etc. between them. You may take play in this direction yourself by altering the home and adjacent area to a medical centre with a few toys and props.

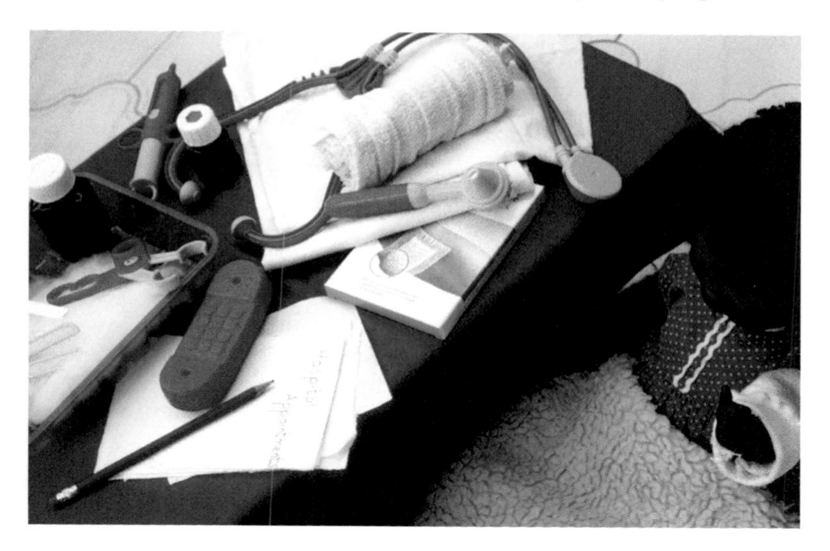

A DOLL, BANDAGE ON ARM, IS BEING ATTENDED TO. FOR SAFETY AND HYGIENE REASONS TOY MEDICAL INSTRUMENTS E.G. STETHOSCOPE, SYRINGE, TONGS, ARE BEST USED ON DOLLS RATHER THAN CHILDREN.

MAKING A MEDICAL OUTFIT

It is easy to make a tabard style medical outfit from white or blue remnant material. Measure your child from shoulder to knee then from shoulder to shoulder. Mark the length and width measurements onto a sheet of folded newspaper.

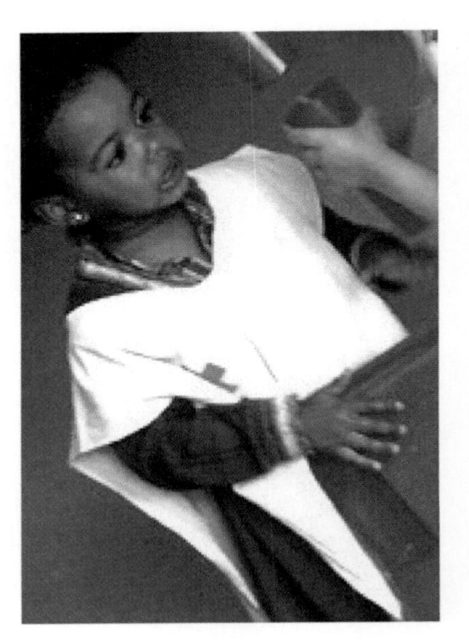

Cut it out, including a semicircle opening for your child's head. Check it fits, pin the template to the cloth then cut out with pinking shears. Attach velcro below the arm positions, allowing room for clothing and finish off by sticking a first aid style cross, in contrasting green or white tape, to the front of the tabard.

MEDICAL EQUIPMENT

- Contents of a good quality toy medical set designed for pre-school children, e.g. stethoscope, syringe, tongs, (safety and hygiene may preclude some items particularly for groups)
- Soft white sponge instead of cotton wool (to prevent adverse reaction to fibres) dampened slightly for authenticity
- Swab dish (genuine article or a clean plastic vegetable/fruit tray) receptacle for the dampened sponge
- Couple of bandages
- Empty packets of plasters and dressings
- Foam mat for the patient to lie on and blankets for warmth

- Administration materials for reception table: two telephones/mobiles (use to make appointments and as a pager) pencils and paper, diary, calendar
- Waiting area with magazines, notice board, child size chairs

MEDICAL CENTRE PRETEND ROLE PLAY

Medical supplies described above can be laid on a low table, tray, upturned plastic crate or toted around in a small bag; in the vicinity a chair, mat and blanket for the patient. Waiting cum reception area set up with equipment described using a child size table, the home area or play unit (refer to chapter eight).

- Medical staff examine, make recommendations/notes, apply bandages, write prescriptions
- Carers wipe wounds, feed and comfort the patient, generally attend to their needs as they wait for the patient to get better
- Hospital/practice administrators make and receive calls, concerning appointments, which they write down in the diary
- Patients and carers sit in the waiting area flicking through magazines having introduced themselves at reception

Hairdressing and Beauty

HAIR TOOLS

Much better than toy versions are real hair accessories, they are more robust and unique. Check that the slides, bows, ribbons, hair-bands, slides, ruffles and so on are not broken or damaged and thoroughly clean previously used hair accessories. Organise them, together with a few clean empty plastic shampoo bottles, (travel size are fun to use too), on a toy trolley, small plastic vegetable rack on castors, tray or low height table.

FOR PLAY AT HOME: A LACY CLOTH COVERS A LOW TABLE; DISCARDED POWDER AND EYE-SHADOW COMPACTS, WITH REMNANTS OF POWDER INTACT ARE READY TO DAB ONTO THE DOLL'S FACE, WITH FRESH BRUSHES AND SPONGE APPLICATORS.

A safety hand mirror (glass free) is a must for your child to hold up for customers to see the finished effect. An old light travel style hairdryer with casing intact, batteries and flex removed is an additional prop or make one using strong cardboard tubing.

Cut out two small tubes, one for the air outlet and the other for the handle and attach together with tape.

HAIRDRESSING PLAY

Your child enjoys rummaging through vanity bags, pulling out hair accessories, arranging them on a trolley and wheeling them around to customers. For hygiene reasons it is best for children to titivate dolls' abundant locks rather than each other's. Settings may preclude hairdressing and beauty play on dolls as well. Experimenting with the host of tools in their arsenal they brush, comb, apply velcro rollers, fix slides, primp and shape. Finally, holding hand-mirrors for their customers, they twist themselves around to see their creations from the customers' perspective. Let them delve into the fabric box to find remnants sufficiently glitzy to go with the dolls' new hairstyles.

BEAUTY ACCESSORIES AND PLAY

Collect a few real cosmetic bags and empty beauty compacts. They come in a wider range of shapes patterns and colours than toy imitations; check they are clean and undamaged. Your child enjoys turning out the contents of the cosmetic bags, (setting them out on a beauty counter too - see chapter eight shop play), arranging them, carrying them around, applying them (onto dolls' faces) and returning them to their bags.

HAIR AND BEAUTY CLOTHES

Hairdressers and beauticians wear stylish plain clothes; a black tabard for the former and white for the latter replicates the look nicely; refer to the medical outfit for instructions on how to make a simple tabard. Add a pocket in the front, for storing tools, by increasing the length of the tabard by 7 to 10 cm. Turn up this allowance, sewing to the tabard sides along the edges. Capes could be made for the dolls, not unlike the real article, from children's shirts. Trim sleeves and collars and button up the new cape at the back.

The World Around

Home and School Play: Times Past

A mob cap and pinafore for a girl, waistcoat and long trousers for a boy, and artefacts unlike anything your child sees now, links her with the past. Settings could temporarily transform the home area with Victorian style clothes and domestic tools such as, washboards, wash tubs and irons. Talk about how hard work in the home was back then compared to now.

Children enjoy imaginative school play. Use chalk, blackboards (tell your child you remember them although they are not used now) and slates for writing if you can acquire them, (your child's grandparents may remember them). Settings may be able to borrow props from their local museum or education authority.

Location

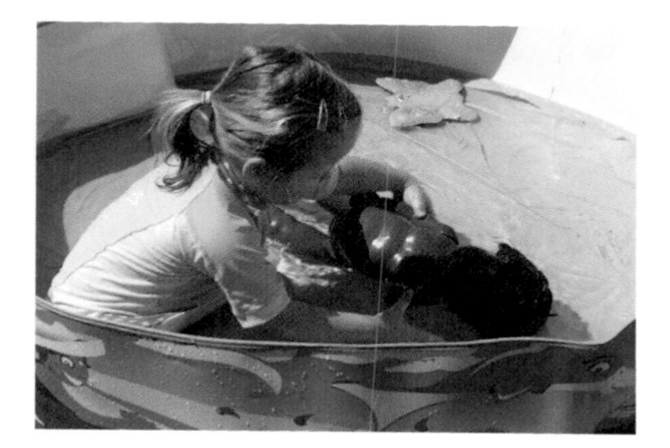

Play can extend beyond the immediate home area; as you supervise, she bathes the doll, outside in summer, sets it in a den home and pushes it in the pram, for a winter walk.

8

Structured Pretend Play

This type of pretend play often revolves around children taking on occupational roles, for example, as a shopkeeper, bank cashier and travel agent. The play may overlap with home play; a visit to the shop entailing a return home to store purchases away, but is generally more defined and structured.

Your child brings to his play what he has observed when out and about. For example, in the post office he sees letters and parcels being weighed, stamps stuck down, money handed over and mailbags collected. Visiting a bank he notices the interchange, the writing and passing of papers, between you and the cashier. His experience, however limited, of how these institutions work enriches and broadens the imaginative role-play versions.

Children are keen to be involved in discussing play ideas, layout and the setting out of equipment. They are thrilled if you have time to join in as well and benefit from your participation. Judge the time to retreat noticing how your time as a customer in their shop, café and so on has enthused them, enhancing the quality of play. Later in the chapter play suggestions point out the props to use, how to organise them and how to play with them effectively.

Layout for Play

A temporary conversion of the home area can be organised, replacing some contents with the required role-play equipment. At settings, a purpose made unit, on castors, or modular panels slotted together to fit requirements is ideal. Alternatively improvise with large boxes (see end of chapter) or strong safe furniture (see overleaf).

A LARGE FREE STANDING, MARKET STYLE WOODEN UNIT, WITH THE ABILITY TO ACCOMMODATE THREE CHILDREN BEHIND THE COUNTER.

At home you can utilise what you already have. Low height occasional tables, with rounded corners, are often just the right height for your child to stand to. Two lightweight bedside tables set apart and covered with a section of strong cardboard make a suitable counter surface. For home use shop style toy units are available; accommodating one child behind the counter they are similar in ethos to toy kitchen centres.

A SMALL DRESSING TABLE/DESK WITH SURFACE AND SHELVES STACKED WITH GROCERY PRODUCTS. THIS TYPE OF FURNITURE IS A SUITABLE HEIGHT, GIVES MORE COUNTER SPACE THAN A HOME PLAY SHOP AND ACCOMMODATES TWO SHOPKEEPERS RATHER THAN ONE.

General Props

The props in this section are relevant to all play situations in the chapter and to avoid repetition are not added to the individual lists of equipment for mini market, café and so on.

Signage

Structured pretend play offers plenty of opportunity for incorporating written signage. Utilise any writing surfaces integrated into play units and, if you have one, a blackboard, wipeboard or magnetic board. Write signs on card, settings could laminate the card or cover with plastic film for durability, then attach to the unit. Discuss names with your child, a shop, for example, might be 'the village store, mini market or corner shop'. For maximum effect, erect the name sign so it is easily visible, hung as appropriate.

THE SIGNS 'OPEN, CLOSED', ARE SUITABLE FOR EVERY SITUATION AS IS A SIGN INDICATING THE BUSINESS E.G. 'HAIRDRESSER'. PERSONALISE SHOPS AND OTHER WORKPLACES E.G. 'JACK'S MINIMARKET', 'HANNAH'S CAFE'. SETTINGS COULD USE THEIR OWN NAME, GIVING A SENSE OF OWNERSHIP, E.G. 'EARLY BIRDS POST OFFICE'.

Dressing up, Accessories and Storage

Children can pick up clothes, hats, handbags, shopping bags, baskets and purses and wallets full of coins from the dressing up area. Other clothes too, according to occupation, e.g. aprons for waiters and chef tabards for cooks. Space is at a premium for me, so I establish storage crates for each play situation and save space by packing smaller items inside larger ones, e.g. plastic fruit and vegetables inside cereal packets. I manage to replenish props, keeping them interesting and fresh for children, without encroaching on space, by throwing things away as they become tired, worn or damaged.

Coins

Keep a store of very shiny coins ready for structured play situations. Grab a handful and arrange in a compartmentalised plastic container, toy cash register or clean supermarket tray. He is not concerned, nor need he be, about the true value of the coins.

Literacy Opportunities

STRUCTURED PRETEND PLAY IS AN IDEAL ENVIRONMENT FOR MAKING MARKS AND WRITING ALPABET LETTERS THAT HAVE BEEN LEARNT.

As cashiers, waiters, administrators and so on children write on scrap paper, in notepads, diaries and calendars. Of course, real banks, offices and surgeries use computers but your child can use computers elsewhere; otherwise he loses the opportunity to write and make marks on paper. Each time pretend role-play is laid out ask your child to see if he can retrieve the appropriate signs and placards and help you put them up. 'We're opening the bank today, see if you can find the 'bank' and 'open' signs.

Number Opportunities

Make use of counting opportunities in pretend shop play. As a customer of a play jewellery shop I frequently sported up to thirty bangles on my arm. I would ask a child to help me count them and noticed whoever it was, whether I counted, they counted or if it was a joint effort they remained fascinated to the end. Currently, I am frequenting a sweet shop selling sherbets, mints, strawberry dips and blueberry candies colourfully represented by plastic pegs, buttons and cotton reels. I'm forever changing my mind. 'There aren't quite enough sherbets for me, shopkeeper, I really need two more.' 'There are too many here, can you take one away please? 'How many sweets have you got for me altogether?

When your child has filled your bag with purchases you can ask, 'How many pennies do I owe you'. He makes up a figure, say five. Pass the coins over saying, 'There's five pennies for you'. You could add, 'May I have two small pennies in change, please'. Count coins as you would bangles, sweets and any other objects. It does not matter at this stage if it is nonsense in real money terms.

Cafe

Your child enjoys arranging the café equipment on the counter. Each time he opens, there is fresh interest for him, as he decides on the menu of the day and selects the food accordingly. He loves you to join him; you are viewed with respect, understanding all this cafe business. He and his friends are wide-eyed as you enter their pretend world; conversing with them and keeping the proceedings flowing; ordering a second cup of coffee, more food then gathering up coins to pay the bill. When you stand back, you realise your time in the café has enthused them, enhancing the quality of their play.

A SMALL PINE DESK, CUTLERY IN THE DRAWER, BECOMES A FOOD SERVING AREA FOR THE CAFÉ. COINS ARE IN A TRAY A MENU AWAITS CUSTOMERS, A NOTEPAD AND PENCIL READY FOR ORDERS.

Café Equipment Suggestions

- Convert the home area, play unit, small desk, or low occasional furniture into a café serving counter; an extra surface may also be needed. Provide a child height table and chairs for customers.

- Essential: toy dinner/tea set, small tray, two phones, pads and pencils (for taking orders), diary (for taking bookings), tablecloth and real shiny coins. Dressing up clothes for customers, aprons and tabards for staff.
- Pictorial and printed menus: introduce different menus, with prices, to suit your collection of play food. Set the customers' mouths watering by drawing or sticking pictures on the menus to help them interpret the written descriptions. Real menus from real cafes also go down a treat.
- Make play dough food (see instructions chapter five modelling materials) to fit breakfast, tea and dinner menus; e.g. for breakfast offer, sausage, fried egg, toast and tomato, for tea tarts and buns and for dinner fish, chips and peas. Make the food chunky with extra-large peas so they do not get lost.
- Use toy plastic food instead of or in conjunction with salt dough food; settings need to purchase good quality plastic food for realism and to withstand wear and tear.
- Change the café into a Chinese or Indian restaurant. Make salt dough naan bread or buy cultural pretend food. Lay out with menus, empty packets of rice, coconut and rice noodles.

Café Staff Roles

Help your child and others engage in café play; pick up some props to chat about, 'What job involves working in this apron?' and 'What job involves answering the telephone?' The manager can take phone bookings, writing them in the diary; he can show customers to their seats and receive payments (see counting mini market). Waiters can lay tables, write down customers' orders, serve food and clear away. Chefs can plate the orders, arranging them on a tray with drinks and napkins, ready for waiters to take away. Customers eat and drink showily with lots of noisy slurping from empty beakers.

CUSTOMERS ENJOY THE BUSINESS OF SITTING, WAITING TO BE SERVED, LOOKING AT THE MENU, ASKING WAITERS FOR THEIR RECOMMENDATIONS, DECIDING ON DISHES AND DRINKS AND LATER CALLING FOR THE BILL AND SETTLING UP.

Bank/Post Office/Office

Play tends to be natural and informal, often an amalgamation of office, bank and post office. To differentiate the roles offer extra equipment e.g. weighing scales for the post office, keys for the bank and logo stamps (use play inked stamps) for the office. Make space for two, behind the counter or desk, maybe three children at settings, putting out an additional table if necessary. It is more productive and interesting, in this situation, apart from deliveries and collections, for children to be working behind the counter than to be customers. Show your interest with casual appearances at the counter.

Equipment Suggestions

DISCARDED UNDAMAGED ITEMS FORM THE BASIS FOR POST OFFICE, BANK AND OFFICE PLAY.

- Furniture: pretend play unit, low occasional table or small desk/dressing table that your child can stand and write at.
- Paper: collect loose sheets, diaries, calendars, notepads, jotters, unwanted stickers (they do nicely for stamps), envelopes, (those enclosed with junk mail and unsealed envelopes from greeting cards are ideal). At home collect scrap paper too, group settings could mention to parents that clean unwanted paper is always welcome.
- Miscellaneous stationery: self-inked business stamps (old clothing - ink may mark), craft/toy stamps, unwanted business cards, pen holders, fancy stationery holders (superfluous once stationery is used).
- Other items: supermarket loyalty cards (they mimic bank debit/credit cards) assorted pencils, key ring with keys (you

have long forgotten what they open). Two phones, balance scales or light household scales, a post box (large red painted box with letter slot cut out) and drawstring bag (pump bag) for a letter sack.

Play

Children enjoy displaying the business and 'open' signs and writing marks and letters on paper which they shuffle fold, stuff into envelopes (children enjoy writing on the envelopes too), then seal. A haphazard exchange of paper may then ensue before it begins all over again. In their roles as cashiers and administrators children like to post their letters and parcels. A child becomes postman, emptying the letters and parcels from the post box into a sack to deliver to the office, bank and home corner. They could occasionally be delivered later, for children to take home to open.

Mini Market

A TOY UNIT FOR SHOP PLAY AT HOME, ACCOMMODATES ONE CHILD BEHIND THE COUNTER AND ONE OR TWO CUSTOMERS.

Equipment Suggestions

STOCK SET OUT ON THE COUNTER AND SHELVES OF A SMALL PINE DRESSING TABLE/DESK WITH REAL MONEY ARRANGED IN A TRAY ON AN ADJOINING BEDSIDE TABLE. THIS ARRANGEMENT ACCOMMODATES TWO SHOPKEEPERS RATHER THAN ONE. THE REAL EMPTY FOOD AND HOUSEHOLD PACKETS LOOK AND FEEL DIFFERENT FROM ONE ANOTHER, AND ARE SATISFYING TO PLAY WITH.

- Save an assortment of empty food and household packets, cleaning thoroughly first.
- Real vegetables, at home only, are a novelty. When you put out the odd piece of real food such as celery and carrots, expect your child to have a nibble - useful if you need to persuade him to eat vegetables.
- Toy plastic pretend food can be worth purchasing, a few pieces of 'fruit and vegetables' and ice cream cones. Settings can order realistic life size examples from an educational supplier. Consider half a dozen pretend eggs too - fun to store in a real egg box, which is easy to replace when tatty.
- Baked salt dough pretend food, see modelling materials chapter 5 for instructions. Buns, tarts, gingerbread men, fairy

cakes, seeded rolls and pizzas, are easy to make and paint and your child enjoys handling them in the bakery section.

- Prices written in numerals on stickers to attach directly to items or on card for placing in front - use the free standing price tickets only occasionally, overused they may interfere with play.
- Grocery orders: Settings can print off order forms for customers to fill in for home delivery (photograph items for sale, organise in list format with photos, names and prices).

Play

Your child takes pleasure in sorting and distributing the stock, from storage crate to shelves. When he is shopkeeper, the shop is, no doubt, an old fashioned grocer; you make a request, he finds the goods and fills your bag. When the roles are reversed, he deems the shop to be self-service! He loves to receive your coins, remind him to give you change. He is not concerned, nor need he be, about the real value of the money.

ARRANGING STOCK ON SHELVES IN A HOME BASED SHOP UNIT.

Shopkeepers find customers are soon back, much to their satisfaction; they are anxious for as much custom as possible. The stock soon becomes depleted and returning purchases to rearrange on the counter is all part of the play. Extra supplies to restock the shop may be required by groups, especially when play extends to setting out purchases on shelves in the home area. For deliveries 'sit in cars' are stacked with goods and driven off to the home area, whether an order form is filled in or not.

TOY CASH REGISTER, WITH COIN STORAGE AND CARD READER. USE REAL MONEY, IT IS MORE EXCITING FOR HIM TO HANDLE NEW, SHINY PENNIES AND HALFPENNIES THAN IMITATION COINS.

Props Inspiration/Themes

Build on your child's previous experiences and trips taken, tales heard, programmes watched. 'Fireman Sam', for example, helps him visualise what a fire officer does, he brings this knowledge to his play (see chapter 6 props).
I set up a line of chairs in a spacious hall, on this train bus or aeroplane passengers enjoy:

- 'All aboard' for embarkation - passengers hopping on
- Finding a seat in the line (or rows) of chairs
- Being at the front steering using hoop as steering wheel
- Taking turns to be passenger, driver, attendant
- Raising the arm (perhaps holding a flag) and bringing it down signalling departure
- Making 'choo choo' noises as the steam train gathers speed

- Working a buffet/refreshment trolley (any toy with storage space) along the line
- Getting off to visit places e.g. safari park, the beach
- Buffing the vehicle to a shine with rag and sponges

LOUIS USES THIS ARRANGEMENT OF LARGE BOXES AS A RECYCLING LORRY WITH A CIRCULAR TRAY FOR A STEERING WHEEL. HE COLLECTS A WASTEPAPER BIN PUTS IT IN THE BACK OF THE LORRY DRIVES OFF TO THE NEXT ONE THEN TAKES THEM ALL TO THE RECYCLING DEPOT. USE A SIMILAR UNIT AS A TELEVISION, THEATRE, SHOP, DEN, DELIVERY VAN, BUS, TRAIN AND SO ON.

Learning Outcomes

Chapters 6, 7 and 8

Personal, The World Around

The world of grown-ups can seem very confusing; imaginary play helps your child make sense of the world and the people in it. He finds out what it is like to be a parent, fire-officer, shopkeeper, when he pretends to be that person. Worries and anxieties e.g. forthcoming visits to the doctor and dentist are alleviated through imaginative play.

- Begins to understand experiences he meets outside the home
- Meets others and joins in imaginative play with them
- Gains in confidence as he interacts with other children in the often complex structures of imaginary play
- Realises self-control is necessary if play is not to disintegrate
- Understands consideration for others and co-operation quickly settles disagreements and smoothes hurt feelings
- Reaches decisions with other children to help play along
- Shares and organises toys and props with other children
- Expresses feelings of annoyance, frustration and tenderness, without repercussions, when playing with toys like dolls
- Attempts things, in imaginative play, he would normally be too uncertain to try yet (on path to self-reliance)
- Repeats pretend play he enjoys, building confidence for fresh challenges
- Concentrates on tasks and goals when thoroughly involved as he is in imaginative play

Language, Literacy

Pretend play provides unforced informal language and literacy opportunities.

- Extends his existing language skills as he communicates with others during imaginative play
- Works hard to express himself clearly to be understood by others during play
- Represents sounds/noises made by vehicles, characters, animals, the elements as he plays
- Makes marks and writes alphabet letters using a wide range of materials (e.g. diaries, pads, envelopes)
- Displays printed signs for structured play situations
- Observes print on play costumes labels, placards, menus etc
- Recognises, over time, some signs and other print forms used as part of imaginary play

Cognitive Processes, Personal Qualities

Quality imaginative play engages your child; it is rewarding for him. He is prepared to think hard, stretching his brain in the process, with what appears to be little effort, in a flexible, creative way to solve problems and move play along.

- Discusses with others, what to play, where to play, how to organise props and allocate roles
- Moves towards abstract thought as he uses symbols to represent things, e.g. threading buttons for sweets.
- Reaches agreement with others as play evolves on how and what should be altered
- Concentrates, giving play his whole attention is natural for him (benefits from increasing ability to sustain attention)
- Pursues play, thinking laterally, as he attempts a fresh approach to familiar things - in a natural unforced way
- Multitasks happily during imaginative play, a position which ordinarily may be irksome or difficult for him

Mathematics

- Counts in pretend play situation e.g. coins, bangles, sweets

- Exchanges coins as a cashier and customer (purchasing and selling) in a range of structured play situations
- Sets out the table with matching place settings in home, café
- Recognises numerals on price tags and menus in shop, café
- Makes marks for numerals in bank, shop, café, home play
- Shares out pretend biscuits etc. between children and toys
- Divides pretend food into smaller amounts, equal portions
- Develops spatial awareness as he rearranges props in the home area, makes dens, negotiates obstacles
- Forms concepts when talking during imaginative play about time e.g. 'We've got to be at the baby clinic for 9 o'clock'

Creativity, World Around, Physical Skills

- Explores, resolves what he has seen as he plays imaginatively
- Appreciates new situations through a variety of make believe
- Prompted by stories heard, to play in exciting imaginary places representing characters, animals and the elements
- Evokes both bygone and modern worlds through his senses; feel, smell of fabrics and props from different eras and places
- Manipulates play equipment and tackles fastenings on dolls' clothes and dressing up clothes developing fine motor skills
- Develops, during active imaginative play, bodily strength, agility, balance and co-ordination as he moves props, runs around, negotiates obstacles, climbs mounds

INDEX

Books 1 and 3

If you enjoyed **Book 2** of **'Play is Child's Work'**, I am sure you would like the other two books in the series: **Books 1 and 3**. They are set out and illustrated in the same way as **Book 2** and the Chapters in each book are listed below. Available via Amazon or to order via good booksellers.

Book 1

1 Resources
Select resources to allow creative and imaginative play full rein

2 Organising Resources
Organise resources – including toys and recycled paraphernalia

3 Personal Qualities
Develop your child's personal qualities and set good behaviour patterns with everyday opportunities and activities

4 Language
Encourage listening and talking during daily routines and special language activities

5 The World Around
Appeal to your child's natural curiosity in the world as you both explore the neighbourhood on foot

6 Towards Literacy
Draw attention to print and pictorial signs, encourage drawing, play matching games – all steps towards literacy

7 Letter Sounds
Arrange, and together with your child enjoy letter sound games, your own alphabet collage, alphabet books and jigsaws

8 Writing
Provide for mark making, make personalised writing books, help your child start writing letters and words

9 Books and Reading
Foster early reading experiences choosing quality books, discussing the pictures - bringing plot and characters alive

Book 3

1 Large Physical Movement
Engage your child in running, climbing, balancing, jumping, pedalling - play bouncing, throwing and aiming games together

2 Fine Physical Skills
Develop your child's fine skills with cutting, lacing, threading

3 Small World Imaginative Play
Select small world toys with imaginative play value, help your child adapt the toys for a range of play situations

4 Construction
Choose blocks, interlocking bricks, recycled materials, rearranging components for various construction activities

5 Technology and Kitchen Science
Guide your child in kitchen science - enthuse her in technology with mechanisms, magnets and computers

6 The Natural World
Appeal to your child's affinity with nature and natural materials to make discoveries, draw conclusions and reinforce concepts

7 Number
Take plenty of opportunities for counting during play, daily routines and simple enjoyable activities using toys and props

8 Measurement, Time and Shape
Introduce the language of measurement, time and shape